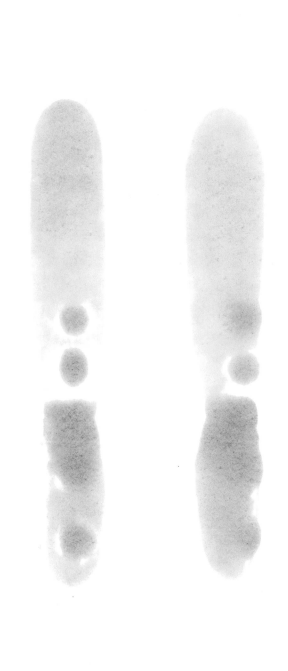

BEGONIAS

BEGONIAS

The Care and Cultivation of Tuberous Varieties

BRIAN LANGDON

CASSELL · LONDON

To Pam, Suze, and Tiddie, the three girls in my life

Text and illustrations © Brian Langdon 1989

First published in 1989 by
Cassell, Artillery House
Artillery Row, London SW1 1RT

British Library Cataloguing in Publication Data
Langdon, Brian
Begonias
1. Begonias Cultivation
I. Title
635.9'3346

ISBN 0 304 32246 6

Produced by Justin Knowles Publishing Group
9 Colleton Crescent, Exeter EX2 4BY

Design: Michael Head
Line illustrations: David Ashby

Typeset by Keyspools Ltd
Printed and bound in Hong Kong

CONTENTS

LIST OF PLATES

INTRODUCTION

The term 'begonia' is often used loosely and sometimes confusingly, and perhaps this is hardly surprising, since at the last count there were well over 2,500 reported species and cultivars in the genus. The term should include any of the species, subspecies, or forms within the genus *Begonia* but in this book it is taken to cover only those many forms with a tuberous root system that are known collectively as tuberous begonias or, in botanical terms, *Begonia × tuberhybrida*, The many other well-known and commercially important groups of begonias – the huge range of fibrous-rooted begonias, the statuesque and ever-popular cane-stemmed begonias, the Rex hybrids with their vividly coloured and elaborately marked leaves, and many others – are all beyond the scope of this book.

My terms of reference, therefore, are to trace the development of tuberous begonias from the discovery of their naturally occurring ancestors in the highlands of South America through to the huge exhibition specimens of today; to give an account of the methods used to raise and grow them; and to help the many thousands of growers all over the world who share my enthusiasm for these most fascinating and rewarding plants to get as much pleasure from them as various generations of my family have done for almost one hundred years.

Since members of my family have devoted much of their lives to working with these plants, the chronicle of events in this century is necessarily something of a family story as well, and I hope readers will bear with me if this occasionally comes through in the narrative. At this point I must pay tribute to the huge debt of knowledge that I owe to earlier generations, from my two grandfathers, C. F. Langdon and J. B. Blackmore, through to my father, the late Allan Langdon, and his younger brother Stephen.

The growing methods described in this book are the distilled results of experience gleaned over many years. They may often appear as daunting and difficult counsels of perfection, especially to the amateur newly approaching begonia cultivation, but there is no short cut to excellence. Again, some readers may disagree with some of my recommendations, claiming to get better results from their own methods. There are, of course, more ways than one of carrying out any given operation, more than one suitable compost to use, and so on, and anyone who has already developed and perfected satisfactory techniques would be foolish to change them – and certainly should not do so because this book says so!

B. J. Langdon

I

ORIGINS, HISTORY, AND DEVELOPMENT

Begonias get their name from Michel Begon (1638–1710), a French colonial administrator and patron of botany. The story of the development of the present-day tuberous varieties is a fascinating one – fascinating as much because of the comparatively short time span involved, in terms of plant development at least, as because of the plant-breeding expertise of the growers responsible. There were no begonias at all described in Miller's *Gardeners' Dictionary* of 1770, though *B. nitida* was imported from Jamaica in that year, and by 1800 only five more species seem to have been in cultivation. From that time onwards, however, a great deal of interest was shown in begonias and plant hunters acting on behalf of the big nurseries of the day and of wealthy private patrons had by 1900 collected another 260 species.

Despite this intense interest in the naturally occurring species, however, there is no record of any hybridizing having taken place before 1860 and so the history of the modern hybrids may be said to date from this point. Begonia species occur in all the continents except Europe and Australasia, but the seven or possibly eight species that figure in our story are all natives of South America. The most famous English nursery in the second half of the 19th century was James Veitch and Sons of Chelsea, on whose staff was Richard Pearce, a dedicated and intrepid explorer and plant-hunter. In early 1859 Veitch sent Pearce first to Chile and Equador and then to Peru and Bolivia. Pearce sent back seed and plant specimens from time to time, including, in 1864, *B. boliviensis*, the first of his begonia speci-

mens, which Veitch exhibited at the 1867 International Horticultural Exhibition in Paris. We think nothing today of sending seeds and even plants long distances by air, but in those days plant material had to suffer trial by prolonged sea voyage and often arrived in poor condition, requiring a further long spell to recuperate and acclimatize to its new surroundings.

B. boliviensis, first described in the 1867 *Botanical Magazine*, is tuberous-rooted and bears small, drooping flowers, cinnabar-red in colour, with very narrow petals about 2in (5cm) long which do not open fully. Its thin leaves are borne on a stem about 2ft (60cm) in height. The modern Pendula forms of begonia that we grow in hanging baskets owe a lot to the thin though supple stems of this species.

Shortly after his discovery of *B. boliviensis*, Pearce moved to La Paz and in 1865 sent back to England two more begonia species, subsequently named *B. pearcei* and *B. veitchii*. The former is a dainty and decorative plant in its own right with bright yellow flowers of 1in (2.5cm) diameter and beautifully marked dark green foliage. *B. veitchii*, with its bright red flowers combined with almost round leaves, quite unlike the other species, was first listed by Veitch in 1869 and marketed as a bedding plant.

While in Peru, Pearce collected a fourth species, *B. rosaeflora*, which Veitch first flowered in 1867. Its flowers were larger than the others, about 2in (5cm) in diameter, varying in colour from white to pale red, but it was in fact little used by the hybridists though it does figure in the parentage of some of the early white varieties.

Pearce left Veitch's employment after his return from this, his first expedition. (He died in 1867, a short time after arriving in Panama to set out on his next expedition.) The firm sent another of their staff, named Davis, to continue where Pearce had left off. Like his predecessor, Davis visited Peru and here he found another important species, later named *B. davisii* in his honour. This is a small plant of dwarf habit with small, brilliant scarlet flowers and glossy leaves. It was used quite extensively in early breeding work, handing on to its progeny an erect flower stem and compact plant habit.

These then were the five species that figured most prominently in the early pedigree of the modern tuberous begonia. For the sake of completeness three others may be mentioned: *B. clarkei*, received from Bolivia in 1867, a species similar to *B. veitchii* in form and colour but of such a delicate constitution that it was little used for breeding work; *B. cinnabarina* with 2in(5cm) diameter, bright red flowers; and *B. parviflora*, a shrubby member of the family that did not cross easily with the other kinds.

The most significant feature of the most important species is the fact that they were discovered growing at altitudes of 10,000ft (3,000m) in forested, mountainous country where, while they were in no danger of frost, the air was cool. This partiality for cool growing conditions remains in the modern hybrids. None of the species mentioned had flowers larger than $2\frac{1}{2}$in (6.5cm) in diameter and all were single in form. Six of them had root systems that were more or less tuberous and these were genetically compatible to the extent that hybrids between them were obtainable easily and in sufficient quantity to encourage nurserymen to develop the strains from these early beginnings.

It is difficult for us now to imagine the great enthusiasm aroused by the arrival of the new begonia species from South America. In France the firms of Crousse and Lemoine, both of Nancy, were extremely active, while in Belgium the work was spearheaded by Van Houtte of Ghent. In England a number of leading firms became involved, amongst them Sutton and Sons, James Carter and Co., Henderson and Sons, and James Bull, but while all these made valuable contributions, it was James Veitch and Sons who made all the early running.

Veitch were fortunate in having as their foreman the very clever hybridist John Seden. Whether he knew very much about the laws of genetics is doubtful, but he was a 'natural' as far as handling and, in particular, raising begonias was concerned, and it was he who was responsible for most of the early work and progress. He raised the first known tuberous begonia hybrid, named *B. × sedeni* after him. Unfortunately neither he nor his employers kept adequate records and we can only surmise the parentage of some of his early crosses. We know that the seed (female) parent of *B. × sedeni* was *B. boliviensis*, but the exact identity of the pollen (male) parent remains in doubt, though it was a species already in Veitch's possession and is thought by some to have been *B. cinnabarina*. The new hybrid was exhibited in 1869 before Britain's Royal Horticultural Society, which

B. × sedeni was the first commercial tuberous begonia hybrid. Raised in 1869 by John Seden, one parent was *B. boliviensis* (the other is not known for certain), and it proved an excellent parent – extremely unusual in an inter-specific hybrid, most of which are sterile.

awarded it a Silver Flora Medal as 'the best new plant shown for the first time in bloom'. Sadly, despite this contemporary euphoria, only avid begonia historians would look at it twice today.

B. × sedeni proved to be a remarkably fertile parent. In this it was exceptional – such interspecific hybrids are almost always sterile – and no doubt Seden was delighted to find his new hybrid more accommodating than he might reasonably have expected. Certainly he made full use of its fecundity both as male and female parent to raise from it many thousands of second-generation hybrids before it became extinct in 1895.

Ten years later, in 1905, a hybrid appeared in the catalogues of the day which may well have been bred from *B × sedeni*, since, to judge from contemporary engravings, it bears a close resemblance to it, and indeed to *B. boliviensis* itself. Called *B. bertini*, it is still to be found in a very few catalogues today, sometimes under the alternative name *B. boliviensis × bertini*. The flower colour is the same orange-scarlet, the petals are very narrow, and it has a tall growth with delicate, sharply pointed leaves.

Another mini-milestone in these early years was one of the very early white varieties, 'Queen of the Whites', which was introduced in 1878 as a selection from *B. rosaeflora* and was chiefly remarkable for being offered by Veitch at over ten shillings (50p), at a time when the average weekly wage of a manual worker was only about three times as much.

Another name entered the field in 1875 – James Laing of Forest Hill. He began by using the three species *BB. boliviensis*, *veitchii*, and *pearcei*, together with four of the available named hybrids. After initial disappointment at the poor quality of his seedlings, he scoured Europe for as many of the latest and best hybrids as he could find, a policy which resulted as early as 1878 in his being awarded by the Royal Horticultural Society the first Gold Medal for begonias, together with a number of First Class Certificates. The tuberous begonia was finally on the map.

Laing's exhibit and the standard of his new seedlings stimulated an almost frenetic activity, with Laing himself growing 200,000 seedlings a year by 1895 and many other nurserymen joining the bandwagon, some as breeders and others purely as stockists of the latest varieties as they appeared. The period between 1875 and World War I was very much the pinnacle, or perhaps the plateau, of begonia cultivation, which became a fashionable cult among the moneyed classes of the day. Begonia one-up-manship flourished as never before or since. The first reported double-flowered begonia was listed by Lemoine in 1876 under the name *lemoinei*. Others followed in quick succession, the going catalogue price being about 15 shillings (75p, $3.50).

But of course, not all begonia enthusiasts were rich. There were many amateur growers who made up in enthusiasm and hard work what they lacked in financial resources. Among them were two men whose names were soon to become permanently associated with begonias – Charles Frederick Langdon and James Barrett Blackmore. Langdon, who was born in 1868 (the year before *B. × sedeni* was raised), was the son of the head woodsman at Newton Park, near Bath, then the seat of Earl Temple of Stowe. He trained as a gardener at Newton Park and later became head gardener to the wealthy vicar of nearby Newton St Loe. It was here that Langdon first came to grow the new cult flower, raising as many as 10,000 seedlings every year. He was of course fortunate that his employer's wealth allowed him to buy the best varieties available and fortunate, too, that he was given much encouragement and a considerable degree of autonomy in the work he loved.

Blackmore was born in 1856 in the same village, Newton St Loe, and was apprenticed to his family's small engineering company in nearby Bath. He had been brought up by his grandparents, who lived in and ran the Crown Inn in Twerton, now a suburb of Bath, and when they died he inherited it and gave up engineering to run it himself. He was passionately fond of flowers and, having built himself a greenhouse in the inn garden, he too was seized with begonia fervour and was soon devoting more and more time to begonias and less and less to the inn, selling plants of his own raising to other enthusiasts and even publishing his own modest list of available varieties.

Langdon and Blackmore often met at local flower shows and, drawn together by their shared love of flowers, and despite a complete difference in temperament, they decided to go into partnership. In 1900 they established Blackmore and Langdon, a firm which, as a private company, continues today. Blackmore, from the proceeds of his sale of the Crown Inn, provided the bulk of the finance; Langdon provided most of the professional horticultural expertise. Starting with their own introductions, which they supplemented by purchases from the pick of other specialists, the new firm rapidly overtook other European begonia growers as the source of the most up-to-date varieties and forms.

As the British firm's fame grew worldwide, so the interest in tuberous begonias of the two French firms, Crousse and Lemoine, diminished; they are now best remembered for their pioneer work in the field of fibrous-rooted, winter-flowering begonias. But Belgian growers in the Ghent/Lochristi region soon realised the potential of begonias as bedding subjects and began to grow them in vast numbers, as they do to this day. They now provide the great bulk of the mass-produced tubers currently marketed.

In the early years of the 20th century the average size of flower was well under 6in (15cm) and consequently public demand quickly centred on the double forms. The early varieties were of poor quality and shape and the stems were weak, but these deficiencies were soon overcome by careful selection of suitable parental varieties. High prices coupled with cheap labour ensured success for the Blackmore and Langdon partnership, until World War I put a very considerable brake on progress – begonia growing gave way to food production and the demand for the few begonias that the firm produced dwindled away to nothing. When the end of hostilities came, those of the staff who were fortunate enough to come home set about rebuilding the enterprise. Gradually orders started to come in again and the breeding programme was revived.

The 1920s and 1930s saw a new trend emerge. No longer were the named varieties of double begonia being bought only by wealthy patrons with a staff of gardeners; now the emphasis was fast turning to the man of modest means who would buy a few tubers every year and grow and attend to them himself. Flower shows throughout the United Kingdom provided the means to publicize the latest varieties. This too was the era of the American millionnaire who had to have the biggest and best and was, until the 1930 slump, prepared to pay large sums for the privilege. This period came to an end with World War II, when, for the second time in the century, the breeding of begonias was interrupted under the pressure of greater events. The firm of Blackmore and Langdon survived the war and the bombing of their nursery in 1942. C. F. Langdon died in 1947, leaving a legacy of many hundreds of plant introductions.

American growers have played their part in the development of the begonia, notably Vetterle and Reinelt and the Brown Bulb Ranch, both of Capitola, California. The Brown Bulb Ranch is much the bigger enterprise, being involved in the mass production of begonia tubers by the million for the chain-store market. Frank Reinelt was the hybridizing genius responsible for the famous Pacific strains of begonias, delphiniums, and polyanthuses that made such an impact in the 1950s and 1960s. He was concerned with the breeding and development of seed strains of uniformly high quality rather than of individual named clones. He achieved great success, but dogged by ill-health, and with no sons or partners to continue his business, he moved to Mexico and spent the last years of his life growing cacti.

Scotland too has long been the home of begonia growers. Scottish amateur growers usually exhibit their flowers on 'boards' rather than as overall plants, and the varieties they have introduced have largely reflected this bias. Their most productive hybridist was the late Alan King, a humble man whose love of the begonia is legendary. He raised a number of excellent varieties, mostly best suited to exhibition on boards, some of which are still widely grown for this purpose.

This, then is the history of the modern forms of tuberous begonia. Little more than a century is a very short while in the history of a garden plant and the begonia's progress from insignificant Andean youngster to belle of the Western greenhouse has been little short of miraculous.

2
RAISING BEGONIAS FROM SEEDS

There are two initial problems about raising begonias from seeds. First, there is the seed itself. Begonia seed is extremely small, with about 70,000 seeds per gram (over 2 million per oz) and this poses difficulties in handling. A retail packet probably contains about 250–300 seeds and more than one amateur has thrown away a packet in disgust thinking that it was empty and others have been convinced they had been sold only dust. Sowing the seeds straight from the packet is likely to result in a very uneven spread, but mixing them with twenty or thirty times their volume of very fine silver sand or vermiculite dust enables an even distribution to be achieved very easily – the pale colour of the carrier, in contrast to the reddish-brown of the seeds, shows exactly where the seeds have been sown so that sowing too thickly may be avoided.

The second difficulty is that of maintaining the required temperature. In the northern hemisphere begonia seeds should be sown in January or early February and require a constant temperature of 18–24°C (63–75°F). Constant really does mean constant – day and night – and at the coldest period of the year, when outside temperatures can be well below freezing, the maintenance of the required warmth is not easy. Small electric propagators are ideal for raising begonia seeds provided they have an effective thermostat and are sufficiently powerful. If the propagator is too low powered and the night is a very cold one, the thermostat may be calling for heat and the elements incapable of answering the demand; then the temperature drops and the seeds or seedlings are ruined.

Seed-sowing composts must be sterile, well-drained, retentive of moisture, and very finely divided (for more detailed information about composts see pages 81–2). Good drainage is achieved by using shallow seed pans, either plastic or clay (but plastic are easier to sterilize), with several drainage holes in the bottom covered by a thick layer of coarse gravel. A layer of compost – 1in (2.5cm) deep is ample – is lightly firmed to a flat surface and the seeds sown. They should not be covered with more compost, since darkness has been shown to inhibit germination. The best conditions are given by subdued daylight; shading from direct sunlight is essential.

By mixing the extremely small seeds with many times their volume of fine silver sand or vermiculite dust even distribution can easily be achieved.

Watering is best carried out by standing the pan in water and allowing the compost to be soaked from the bottom until the surface is moist without any disturbance of the seed. Let the pan drain thoroughly, and on no account let it stand indefinitely in water. A proprietary mist or fogging unit is useful and permits controlled moisture levels, but this is something of a counsel of perfection and most amateur growers will settle for covering the pan with a small pane of glass or placing it in a polythene bag. In the latter case, if it is moist when bagged there should be no need to water again until removal of the bag after germination.

Germination is usually evident, at least with a magnifying glass, from seven to ten days after sowing. The surface of the seeds will be seen to have ruptured and minute flecks of green will be visible. It is at this stage that the pan should be removed from the polythene bag, if this technique has been

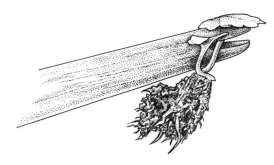

A seedling lifted from the seed pan in the fork of a thin sliver of wood, a method of handling the very small plants that is far less damaging than using fingers. The seedling can be lowered into a hole previously made ready for it in the pricking-out compost, which should then be firmed around it.

In suitable conditions, begonia seeds will show the first signs of germinating between seven and ten days after sowing. They will have reached this size in about a month, and about a week later will be at an ideal size for pricking out into boxes.

used, or from the mist. The most difficult part of the operation will have been completed and the temperature parameters from then on will be a little less critical, a minimum of $13\,^{\circ}$C ($55\,^{\circ}$F) being acceptable. With careful husbandry the seedlings will start to grow quite rapidly, but vigilance is still necessary and any patches of damping-off fungus must be

treated immediately – a proprietary fungicide such as Rovral is suitable.

After about four weeks the young seedlings will be ready to prick out, a process for which even the most elegant human fingers are quite unsuitable. The leaves will be about $\frac{1}{4}-\frac{1}{2}$in (0.6–1.3cm) in diameter, extremely fragile, and very easily damaged and the best method of moving the seedlings involves making a very simple tool for the purpose. Take a sliver of wood about 6in (15cm) long and the shape of a flattened pencil; sharpen one end to a blunt point and carefully cut the other to a bevelled edge with a V-shaped nick in it. The pointed end is used to loosen the compost around the seedlings and the tool

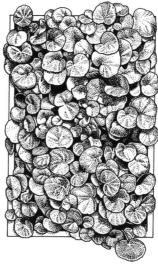

A month or so later, the box of pricked-out seedlings will have developed into robust little plants like these and be ready for a further move.

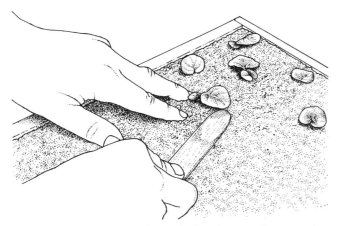

Transplanting into boxes about 2in (5cm) apart. Great care must be taken to handle the seedlings carefully at all stages as the young growth is extremely tender and very brittle.

is then reversed and the V placed under the seed leaf so that the young plant may be lifted clear with its root system dangling. It can then be lowered into a small hole made in the pricking-out compost by the tool's sharp end, and the compost gently firmed around it.

The seedlings should be placed about 1in (2.5cm) apart each way using a fine compost (see page 82). The optimum temperature will be about 15°C (60°F) and watering from this point onwards may be by overhead spray, using as fine a rose as possible.

As growth proceeds a further move will become necessary. The timing of this will be governed by the degree of crowding of the seedlings, which at no time must be allowed to become drawn or 'leggy'. It is likely to be about ten weeks after sowing and should be into seed trays sufficiently deep to accommodate the extra amount of root that the now rapidly growing plants will produce.

At this stage the decision must be made, if it has not been made earlier, whether the seedlings are to be grown under cover in pots or used for outdoor bedding. If the former, then the young plants are potted when ready and treated as described in the next chapter, Raising Begonias from Tubers. However, because there is considerable variation of quality, size, colour, and shape among plants raised from seeds, seedling begonias are recommended for bedding purposes where massed colour is the primary consideration and the quality and size of individual flowers is of much less importance.

For bedding, therefore, the young seedlings are probably best potted into 3in (7.5cm) or 3½in (9cm) pots, but this is not always possible and it is perfectly acceptable to plant out into flowering positions direct from the seed trays. Either way, however, the plants must gradually be hardened to outdoor conditions or their tender growth, used as it is to the warm hospitality of a greenhouse or conservatory, will be badly damaged. A cold frame, if available, is ideal for this purpose, initially with the lights on and minimal ventilation, then with progressive exposure allowed by removal of the lights, first during daytime only and later throughout the 24 hours. In the absence of a cold frame it is advisable to reduce the greenhouse temperature and then, after a week or two, to stand the pots or boxes outside, first in a sheltered position and then alongside the flower bed, taking them in at night for the first week or so. This is a wearisome but worthwhile chore – nothing is worse than having a bed of newly planted begonias spoiled by a spell of hot sun or a cold wind solely because of inadequate acclimatization.

Although their ancestral home is in high mountainous places, begonias are extremely sensitive to frost. They should on no account be planted in the open until all danger of frost has passed, which means deferring planting until late May or early June at the earliest.

The bed itself should be in an open position – while a certain amount of shade is acceptable, full shade or under trees is not. Proper preparation of the soil is important. If possible some form of humus should be dug into light soils to improve water-retention. Well-rotted animal manure is ideal and if this can be dug into the bed two or three months before planting then the plants will be happy indeed. But this is available only to the chosen few – most of us will have to make do with fertilizer out of a packet raked into the top few inches of soil a day or two before planting. The lighter the soil, the more important it is to provide some form of humus. Garden compost should not be despised for begonias, but peat should be used with restraint – it certainly retains moisture and helps root formation, but if it once becomes really dry it is extremely difficult to wet again.

The actual planting requires great care to see that as few of the roots as possible are broken. Some tearing is inevitable when the plants are taken from the boxes and separated from each other, but damage is minimized if the seedlings have been potted prior to bedding. The plants should be set about 10–12in (25–30cm) apart both ways with the ball of root about 2ins (5cm) below the soil level. Water them in immediately and generously, to ensure minimum shock and maximum resettlement speed. Many growers add a mulch of some form of humus after planting, but – unless the soil is very light, sandy, or limy – this is unnecessary provided that the surface of the soil is moved regularly, as when hand-weeding or hoeing, and watering is copious.

If plants have been insufficiently hardened before planting, or if they have been grown under crowded conditions, their first exposure to hot sun can cause severe scorching of both leaves and stems. Lesions will appear on the stems, which tend to shrivel, and round, pale brown markings will disfigure the leaves and may be sufficiently severe to cause them to drop off. The risk of scorching is greatly increased if the plants are dry at the root at the time of exposure, because scorching is due to localized dehydration of the leaf and stem tissues, so generous watering is a safeguard. There is no cure for scorching except time, and plants are rarely so badly affected that they will not gradually become acclimatized.

Begonias are very floriferous; left to their own devices they will tend to produce their first flowers when the plants are quite small. This is too early for their own good, so it is important that the first flowers are removed at an early stage. Whether the plants are ultimately destined for bedding or for greenhouse cultivation, they should be disbudded so that the resources of the plants can build up before the exhausting process of flower production is allowed to proceed. Disbudding will result in larger plants with more and bigger flowers and a better all-round performance. It entails the removal of the first two or three flower stems to appear, so that the plants are not allowed to flower until about early August. When the plants are finally permitted to flower, there is no need to remove the smaller flowers on either side of each large, central flower as is done in the case of plants grown for exhibition purposes (see page 19) as the overall mass of flower is of more importance in the case of bedding plants than the excellence of individual blooms.

While begonias are very tolerant of soil type, the one thing they really dislike is to be dry at the root, so that it is almost impossible to overwater bedding begonias growing in the open ground. In some wet seasons no watering at all may be necessary after the initial post-planting soak, but if weather conditions do render watering necessary a good drenching is much better than a light freshening, which will only encourage roots to the surface, where they are much more prone to shrivelling in any subsequent dry spells.

Given an average season, tuberous begonias will flower from August until the first autumn frosts blacken the foliage. These early frosts are unlikely to be hard enough to penetrate the ground and menace the tubers, but they can be taken as a signal to lift the plants. The longer the plants are kept growing, though, the better prepared the tubers will be for their dormancy, so, if there are no frosts, wait until November. Then the plants should be cut down to within about 4in (10cm) of ground level and lifted with a fork, taking care not to damage the tubers in the process. Correct end-of-season treatment is essential if the tubers are to last the winter in good condition (see page 20). Once lifted, the tubers, each with its ball of root, should be kept in an open box in a frost-proof place and treated in the same way as the greenhouse types (see pages 20–21).

Of course, what goes for bedding begonias is equally valid for all begonias grown out-of-doors with little or no protection from the elements, whether in urns, tubs, window boxes, or large pots on the patio. Container-grown begonias are, however, even more vulnerable to drying out in hot weather.

3
RAISING BEGONIAS
FROM TUBERS

Unquestionably, the cheapest way of raising begonias is from seeds, despite the cost of maintaining the necessary high temperatures. But growing from tubers is certainly the easiest way. Tubers are commercially available in large numbers. They are produced mainly in Belgium, where some millions are produced annually, in other countries of continental Europe, and in the United States of America. British growers account only for the tiniest fraction of the world output.

Continental European and American growers concern themselves with breeding towards uniformity of colour, of growth, and of size of tuber. British raisers are more concerned with size and quality of flower combined with plant vigour, and are continually striving after improvements in these characteristics; they cater exclusively for the high-quality market.

When purchasing tubers, therefore, it is important to decide in advance just what is required. For bedding purposes, where quality of individual flower is of limited importance, bedding-quality tubers are ideal, and the recently introduced Non-Stop range in particular is quite excellent. But for greenhouse or conservatory cultivation, where the full potential of the plant can be realized under controlled growing conditions, the higher-quality tubers are recommended – ideally the named varieties, because these alone are capable of giving the very best results. If loving care is to be lavished on plants and valuable greenhouse space devoted to them, it makes sense to grow plants that repay the effort with large, high-quality flowers.

All varieties, whether ultimately named or not, start their life as seeds, but as begonias do not come completely true from seed – even plants from the same cross can sometimes vary considerably – no two unnamed varieties will be identical. If, however, a given plant is propagated by cuttings or other vegetative means ('cloned', to use modern parlance) then each cutting is part of the original and will be in every way identical to it. Propagation in this way is time-consuming and labour-intensive and is only worthwhile if a given seedling is outstanding in some respect – size of flower, an unusual colour, or whatever – but if the expense is warranted a stock can be built up and a new named variety born. In practice, therefore, named varieties represent the elite of the race – they would not otherwise have been worth propagating.

Dormant tubers as purchased may be started into growth in the northern hemisphere at any time from early January to early May, but unless required in flower very early or very late in the season they should be started into growth in February or March in a warm greenhouse, whether they are destined for bedding or for greenhouse cultivation. If no heated greenhouse is available, an unheated one is perfectly adequate, though starting will have to be delayed until late March. If greenhouse facilities are lacking, a cold frame will suffice, the tubers being started into growth in April for flowering in mid-August. In the absence of any covered facilities at all, dormant tubers may be planted into the open ground $2-2\frac{1}{2}$in (5–6cm) deep in late April; clearly there must be some risk of frost in such cases, especially if the

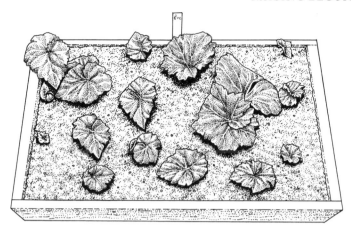

Do not expect all tubers to start at the same time, even if they are all of the same variety. Some will be ready for their first potting before others have even begun to sprout, so it is unlikely that all the tubers can be potted at the same time.

tubers come through the soil quickly, but many people find the risk acceptable and achieve excellent results by growing their bedding begonias from tubers in this way.

With regard to timing, it may be reckoned that in a heated greenhouse it will take about four and a half to five months to bring a tuber to flowering. Tubers destined for bedding, started in a greenhouse and later planted in the open, will take five to five and a half months. The exact timing will depend on many variables, not least the weather and other local conditions.

Whenever started, the procedure is the same for the humblest bedding tubers and the finest named varieties. Tubers should be started in seed trays that are at least 2–2½in (5–6cm) deep. They should be buried with their tops uppermost (the top can be recognized because it bears a large round scar from the remains of the previous season's stem). The tops should be covered by the compost. Tubers produce roots from the whole of their surface and if a tuber is not completely buried it will not produce its full complement of roots, thus diminishing its subsequent performance. In addition, embryo shoots emerge more easily from the tuber if the area where they are produced, that is round the scar, is made moist and soft.

Suitable composts for starting and growing are discussed in chapter 8, but begonia tubers, unlike seeds, are very tolerant and neither compost nor temperature is critical. A temperature of 18°C

(63°F) is ideal, but tubers can be started in the same propagator as seeds if required, while if the temperature falls as low as 13°C (55°F) the tubers will still start but will of course do so rather later.

Healthy tubers in optimum conditions will soon begin to sprout, but some always take longer than others, even in the case of tubers of the same variety, so that it is rarely possible to pot all tubers at the same time, some being ready for a move before others have even begun to shoot. Small tubers will produce only one shoot, but larger ones may well produce two or even three shoots at this stage, so this is the time to decide whether to grow the plants on one or two stems. Most should be grown as one-stem plants, but one or two of the biggest, most vigorous tubers with large complements of root may be allowed to produce two stems, provided the shoots are strong and about 2in (5cm) apart. If any of the named varieties produce more than one shoot the opportunity may be taken to remove any surplus shoots as cuttings (see chapter 5) and this should be done when they are 2–3in (5–7.5cm) tall.

Once tubers have started and growth is between 2 and 4in (5 and 10cm) high they are ready for their first potting. As they are lifted from the trays the amount of root each tuber has made will be apparent. This is important as it is this which should determine the size of pot into which they should go, typically a 4in (10cm) or possibly 5in (12.5cm) size.

A tuber may refuse to start for a number of reasons. It may simply be slow. This is usually obvious on careful examination – the beginnings of a shoot may just be visible, or one or two thin roots. In this case it should be carefully replaced in the compost and impatience curbed. If a non-starting tuber is perfectly sound and the flesh pink when scratched it may simply be that it is being kept too cool (at night possibly?) or too dry – a tuber in the corner of a box can be overlooked when watering and may not get its full quota of water. But if the tuber tissue looks brown then rotting has set in, possibly because an unsuitable compost has been used, while if is is pale brown and mushy then it has almost certainly become frosted. In any event, one or two failures in a batch of tubers must be expected every season – nobody gets through without a small percentage loss.

At one time there was a great debate on the relative merits of clay and plastic pots, but this has now largely subsided and the vast majority of growers have settled for plastic. The main difference is that clay pots are permeable to air and water while plastic are not. The relevance of this is that plants assimilate air as well as water through their roots and clay pots allow the roots to 'breathe', so clay pots are more forgiving while plastic pots are more demanding. Both give excellent results but, as we shall see, it is easier to overwater when using plastic pots, because they are entirely non-absorbent and non-porous. On the other hand, pots made of plastic are easier to clean and provide less in the way of cover for bacteria, fungal spores, and other microscopic pathogens. These are the differences; choose whichever you find most suitable to your own methods.

Watering is undoubtedly one of the most important and most difficult operations in the cultivation of any plant, and begonias are no exception. The basics of the operation of course are to give the plants the amount of water they require when they need it, but this means being able to tell when a plant is dry. Clay pots can be tapped with the knuckle to see if they 'ring', in which case they are dry, or give a dull sound, in which case they are wet, but this rough-and-ready test which served gardeners well for centuries can hardly be applied to plastic pots. Nor can feeling the top surface of the compost with a finger – it may appear dry but be moist lower down. The only valid test is the weight test: if two identical pots are filled with compost, one allowed to become dry and the other kept moist, picking them up in turn will soon demonstrate the effectiveness of this test, the wet one being very much heavier than the dry one. Using this test with pot plants will quickly indicate the degree of wetness of a compost and while the two pots can be kept as reference standards to begin with they can soon be dispensed with as the novice becomes accustomed to making his own judgments.

The other important aspect of correct watering is how much to give at a time. As we have seen, plants absorb air as well as water through their roots and if the compost is kept uniformly wet at all times air will be driven out and, especially in plastic pots, the roots will drown. It is much better, when the compost becomes dry, to give a good soaking and then to refrain from further watering until it becomes dry again, repeating the soaking/drying, soaking/drying routine throughout the plant's growing season. Whether the watering is from the top or the bottom is immaterial; it is the amount given and when it is given that matters.

A further variable is provided by the amount of root the plant has made. If it is well rooted and gives every indication of being a normal, healthy plant then water may be given more generously than to a plant whose root complement is less than average; the rule must always be, 'If in doubt, don't'. Remember, far more plants are ruined by overwatering than by underwatering.

If the potted begonias are required for bedding purposes, they should be kept in their first pots and planted in the open when frost danger is past (as described on page 14). If they are better tubers intended for greenhouse or the conservatory, their treatment will diverge from this point on.

Final potting, that is, potting of the plants into the pots in which they will spend their flowering season, should take place when the nutrients in the first potting have been used by the plant and this is best determined by tapping the individual plants out of their pots. If the roots are running round the sides of the pot, are already beginning to form a mat at the bottom, and are reaching up towards the top of the compost, then the plant is in ideal condition for its final potting. The compost used should be the same as for the first potting (see page 82) and the final pot size will depend on the vigour of the root system and its general condition – typically a plant from a 4in (10cm) pot should be moved to a 6in (15cm) and one from a 5in (12.5cm) to a 7in (18cm). A generous watering after the move to consolidate the compost with the root ball should be followed by only sparse watering until new roots have pushed out into the fresh compost and the plant is growing away strongly again.

As growth proceeds, there are three important chores to perform. First, flower buds will start to form and these must be removed until the plants have built up into good, strong specimens that are capable of standing the strain on the plant system that flowering imposes. If begonias are allowed to flower prematurely not only will the plants themselves be held back but the flowers will be of poor quality – possibly semi-double in form – and of small size. Far better to sacrifice the first few buds and build up the plants to the point where they will take flowering in their stride, rewarding the grower's patience with the most vivid display of colour known to the plant kingdom.

There is another form of disbudding, however, which consists of removing the side flowers from a given cluster. Tuberous begonias produce their flowers in groups of three at the end of a single stem; the largest one is the central male flower and on either side of this are produced either two female flowers or one female and another male (double) flower. (Female flowers are single in form and are distinguished by the triangular-shaped seed capsule behind the petals.) In order to allow the central, male flower to develop its full potential the two subsidiary flowers should be removed, and the earlier this is done the greater the effect on the remaining bud. Great care is essential because the bud tissues are very brittle and it is all too easy when removing the two smaller buds to snap off the middle one by mistake.

The second chore is staking. One of the characteristics of the cultivated begonia, inherited from its *B. boliviensis* ancestor, is that its growth is asymmetric – that is, there is a definite 'back' and 'front' to the plant, the flowers and leaves tending all to point one way. With the large-flowered double varieties, therefore, the sheer weight of flower will tend progressively to topple the plant unless it is suitably staked. This is best done with pointed wooden stakes about $\frac{1}{2}$in (1.25cm) square and about 20in (50cm) long – or up to 24in (60cm) if the variety is tall growing. The stake should be inserted into the compost about $2-2\frac{1}{2}$in (5–6cm) away from the stem (so as to avoid damage to the tuber) and angled about ten degrees away from the stem; its point should go all the way to the bottom of the pot. This enables the stem and the stake to be drawn together when rings of a suitable tie (a flat tie that will not cut into the soft stem) are added as growth proceeds. The first tie can be made about 6in (15cm) from compost level, a

second and possibly a third being added as necessary. It is often good practice to allow the side shoot produced in the angle between the stem and the first leaf to develop, because this helps to produce a well-furnished and balanced plant, and when this produces a flower it also will require a tie to the stake to hold it in position. But, however many flowers a plant produces, one stake at the back of the main stem should be sufficient.

The third chore is feeding. Because any pot-grown plant has by definition to subsist from a very restricted root run, it will, if its root system is healthy, soon exhaust the nutrients already in the compost. Then supplementary feeding will be required, but not before – *never* feed a plant until it has used up the nutrients already in the compost. Even then, *never* exceed the manufacturer's recommended dosages. Manufacturers naturally want to sell as much fertilizer as they can and their recommendations can be taken as upper limits for plants in full growth with vigorous root systems; don't add a bit for luck or use the preparation more frequently than the instructions indicate. If you do you will do more harm than good, even if the harm falls short of actual root damage and leads only to excessively soft growth and predisposition to diseases such as stem rot. Any general proprietary fertilizer that has a balanced formula will be excellent, preferably a fully soluble one prepared immediately before use. Never use one that is over-rich in nitrogen – an unbalanced fertilizer will lead to unbalanced growth – and never feed a tuberous begonia after the end of August or it will be maintained in growth beyond the point when it should be starting to go to rest (see page 20).

Time and attention devoted to begonias will be amply repaid. A well-furnished double begonia at a flower show, carefully, indeed lovingly, grown and bearing up to six or more large flowers of perfect shape, is a sight to arouse the admiration of all and to give its grower immense satisfaction. Such specimens are not the monopoly of the professional nurserymen. Professional exhibits may be the more spectacular, because of the sheer numbers of plants the professional is able to bring to shows, but plant for plant the amateur can and often does outdo him.

4
TREATMENT AFTER FLOWERING

'After flowering, begonias should be cut down, the pots laid on their sides under the greenhouse staging, and dried off for the winter' – this, or something like it, is the advice still given in too many gardening books. It is wrong in every detail. In the first place, the end of the flowering season is far from the end of the growing season and witholding water at this stage, when the plants are exhausted after producing all those large flowers, will impede their recovery and prevent the tubers building up the resources to tide them over their winter dormancy. Amateurs who claim that they are unable to keep their tubers over the winter have almost always treated their plants in this way and have ended up with hard, shrivelled remains that were in effect killed the previous autumn by being forced into premature dormancy in a debilitated condition and with their stamina at a low ebb.

After they have flowered, tuberous begonias should be allowed to continue growing gently. They should not be fed and all buds should be removed, but they should be watered – until the plants indicate of their own accord when they are ready to go to rest. Water should not be lavished too freely or this will kill off the roots, but plants should be given water as and when they require it, which will not, of course, be as frequently as when they are in full flower in hot weather at the height of the season. The plants indicate unmistakably that they are ready to go to rest when their foliage begins to turn yellow. If they have been given no supplementary feeding after the end of August this is likely to be at any time from mid-October through to Christmas. Sometimes a few plants retain green foliage at this late stage, and these must be cut down anyway, whether they are strictly speaking ready or not, but this extreme does not invalidate the rule that plants should not be forced into premature dormancy. All this, of course, applies only to pot-grown begonias that are frost-protected; in the case of bedding begonias in the open it is likely that frost will take a hand and other criteria apply as already described.

When the leaves start to turn yellow, therefore, the plants may be cut down to within about 6in (15cm) of compost level and all water withheld. They should be taken out of their pots and placed

When the foliage begins to turn yellow and die back at the end of the season, the plants should be cut down to within a few inches of pot level and water withheld.

A box of bedding begonias lifted at the end of the season with some soil attached and the stems cut down to about 6in (15cm). The tubers are loosely spaced so that air can get to them.

loosely in a single layer in a box on the greenhouse bench – the idea is to let the air get to the compost and dry it out gradually so that it can be worked away easily from the tubers in due course. After a week or two it will be found that the stems gradually fall away segment by segment, leaving just the tuber with the remains of the compost sticking to the roots. Most of the roots will by this time have died, though any more fleshy roots that have not done so should be allowed to remain. In some cases the last remnant of stem will prove stubborn and will have to be either snapped away with the thumb or, if that fails to dislodge it, cut away very carefully with a pointed knife. It is however important that it be removed, whichever method is chosen, because if it is permitted to remain it may easily become a focus of rotting and disease during dormancy.

When considering how to store tubers for the winter, it is important to realize the principle involved; conditions have to be such that the tubers do not become so dry or warm that they shrivel and lose weight, nor so wet and cold that they either rot or, worse still, become frosted. It is not enough just to say that they should be stored in a frost-proof place – that is obvious enough. It is the maintenance of the proper moisture equilibrium that, coupled with the correct treatment after flowering and proper harvesting procedure, will ensure that tubers come through their dormant period with the very minimum of losses. In practice one of the best ways to store tubers is to keep them in a plastic bag in the salad compartment of a domestic refrigerator; the constant temperature of about 5°C (40°F) is ideal. They should be quite dry when put into the bag, so that they do not sweat. For larger quantities old dry potting soil is an excellent storage medium, but the tubers should be inspected at regular intervals for any signs of rotting. In this way all tubers should remain in sound, plump condition until the time comes round to start them into growth again.

Although it would appear from the above that a tuber, treated in the appropriate way and given conditions to its liking, should have an almost indefinite life, in fact, after some years (which may be as few as seven or as many as fifteen) it becomes so large that it is unmanageable. Its tissues also become hard and almost woody and the surface develops a corky texture so that the amount of root it is capable of producing is severely restricted. Well before this pensioning-off stage it should be discarded (though not before tuber-cuttings have been taken – see page 22) and the space given over to younger, more vigorous stock better capable of giving good results.

5

PROPAGATION

Broadly speaking, with any plant, there are two basic means of propagation – sexually from seeds and asexually by vegetative means. Progeny derived from seeds inherit some or other of their parents characteristics and, except in the case of line-bred strains (Fɪ hybrids), this means that they do not come true from seeds. There are only a very few Fɪ strains of tuberous begonias, although these include the excellent Nonstop bedding forms. In order to increase stock of an individual variety, therefore, where exact reproduction of every characteristic is necessary, seeds are quite unsuitable and asexual, or vegetative, means of propagation must be used. These may be sub-divided into propagation by cuttings, by division, and by tissue culture, but all three have in common that they utilize a piece of tissue and from it build up small plants identical in every respect to the original. This is the means by which stocks of named varieties are built up by nurserymen or enthusiastic amateurs, and we will consider each of the three techniques in turn.

Division of Tubers

This involves cutting large tubers into individual pieces, each of which must have a shoot. Usually the division will be made shortly after the tuber has started into growth, when it is already clear that at least two strong shoots are present. Each piece of tuber should also have a good complement of root. The cut must be made with a really sharp blade, otherwise the tuber tissue will be torn and subsequent pathogen infection be that much more likely. In fact the main objections to tuber division as

a viable means of propagation are that the tuber not only irrevocably loses a portion of its root system, but that the cut surface may act as a host area for bacteria and similar organisms however cleanly the cuts are made. So far from doubling the stock, both pieces may be lost, though dipping the cut surfaces in a mild fungicide (Benlate may be used for this) minimizes the chance of fungal infections. Even so, it is much better, if an old tuber produces two or more shoots, to wait until they are about 2–3in (5–7.5cm) long, remove them, and treat them as basal cuttings in the way described below.

Propagation by Cuttings

There are two kinds of cuttings – basal cuttings and stem cuttings. Basal cuttings are produced from the tuber surface as just described and stem cuttings from the lower leaf axils, that is, the angles between the leaf stalks and the main stem. In either case it is essential that a very sharp blade be used to remove them; a scalpel-like instrument with a narrow, triangular blade is excellent.

When taking basal cuttings the cut must be made as close to the tuber surface as possible. It is not necessary to include a 'heel' of tuber tissue, but the little ring of tiny sheath-like leaves at the base of the shoots must be included as it is these that protect the all-important 'eye(s)' from which growth in the following season will come and without which the cuttings are unlikely to root.

Stem cuttings, while less easy to take than basal cuttings, are usually more prolifically produced; they appear in the lower leaf axils while the upper

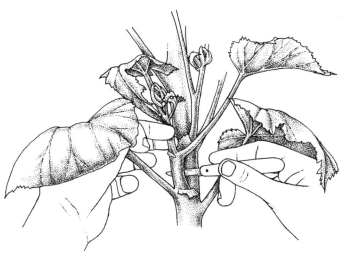

The removal of a suitable cutting making two strokes with a sharp, narrow-bladed knife, one stroke down the main stem, as here, and the other along the top surface of the leaf stalk. The wedge shape ensures the inclusion of the all-important 'eye' or embryo shoot, without which the cutting will not root; without it, the cutting is useless.

axils produce flower stems. The same basic principles apply and it is vital to include the small eye at the very base of the cutting. This is almost impossible to accomplish by making a single cut across the bottom of the cutting, and the easiest way is to make two separate cuts at right angles to one another, one directly down the main stem, continuing into the base of the cutting, and the other along the top of the leaf stalk so as to meet the bottom of the vertical cut. The cutting will come away cleanly, with a wedge-shaped base and with the small growth eye intact, with its protective, vestigial leaf. The wound on the

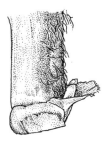

The base of the cutting must include the small 'eye', which will provide the future growing point when the cutting has rooted and a small tuber has formed.

parent plant will quickly heal and after a week or two will have formed a coating of callus tissue to protect itself – consequently there is no need to give it any other protection.

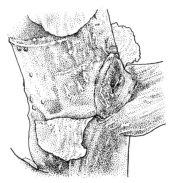

The leaf axil clearly showing the point from which the wedge-shaped cutting has been taken.

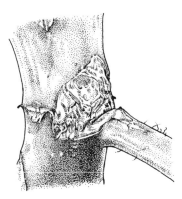

The scar left by the removal of the cutting will dry and seal itself with callus tissue of its own accord after a week or two.

Whether of basal or stem origin, the cuttings must be rooted in compost (see page 82) with their bases about 1in (2.5cm) below compost level, in a humid atmosphere and at a temperature of 18°C (63°F). Some growers use a rooting hormone, some a rooting hormone and fungicide mixed, and others use neither – if the conditions are right the cuttings will root anyway. A misting or fogging system will produce the high humidity that reduces moisture loss through transpiration to a minimum but, failing this, a small propagator will be perfectly satisfactory. At the height of the season cuttings will take about three to four weeks to root and during this period it is important to see that the compost is kept moist but not too wet. Unlike plants growing in pots, cuttings require an even moisture content to be maintained in the compost. This is because they have not yet produced any roots which can 'breathe' and the overriding consideration is to prevent them suffering from dehydration and from rotting at the base brought about by an airlock in the vascular

Cuttings are rooted either singly, as here, or plurally in boxes, in a light, well-drained compost. If you are using small clay pots, it is advantageous to insert the cutting at the side of the pot where the porosity of the clay helps to maintain good drainage in the immediate vicinity of the rooting area.

system at the bottom of the cutting and the entry of bacteria.

After about five or six weeks the rooted cuttings may be removed from the propagator or mist system, stood out in a light, airy position, and looked after in the normal fashion until the end of the season. If they were taken very early in the season and are from particularly vigorous varieties they may become large enough to warrant potting into 4in (10cm) or even 5in (12.5cm) pots, but otherwise they should remain in the pots in which they were rooted. By the time they are harvested in November or December they will have made tubers, generally about the size of a small walnut. The details already given for harvesting and storing apply equally to these so-called 'cutting tubers' but, because they are so much smaller than their older brothers, they are much more vulnerable and great care has to be taken during their dormancy to see that they do not shrivel or come to any harm, though despite every attention losses are always greater among these small tubers.

Begonia rex and other fibrous and rhizomatous begonias can be propagated by leaf cuttings, that is,

small sections of leaf which have been trimmed and set in compost. Sadly, tuberous begonias are not amenable to rooting in this way and despite hormone rooting powders, mist techniques, and every encouragement they remain implacable in their refusal to co-operate.

Unless, that is, the grower has access to all the facilities of a modern plant laboratory. Then very small pieces of plant, sometimes as little as a single cell, can, given the right chemical medium and controlled environment, be made to undergo cell division at a rapid rate. They produce shoots which, when transferred to a second medium, develop roots and become to all intents and purposes miniature plants which can be potted and which, after a period of weaning, will grow into full-sized plants. This is the tissue-culture method, which was supposed to render all the old ways obsolete. Perhaps one day it will, but laboratories with the necessary equipment are expensive to set up – tissue culture has to be carried out in a totally sterile environment; any endemic bacteria, of which begonias seem to have plenty, have first to be removed; the cells to be cultured have to be dissected under a microscope in a current of filtered air; and each species, often each variety, requires its own individual media formulae for multiplying and rooting. Despite promising initial progress a number of professional tissue-culture laboratories have floundered and the bulk of the begonias offered today are still propagated by the time-honoured macro-methods, honed as they have been by years of experience. One day, probably sooner rather than later, the keen amateur will have his own small laboratory in the same way as keen photographers have their darkrooms, but that is not the position yet.

6

PESTS AND DISEASES

One of the major advantages of the tuberous begonia over many other pot plants is that it is prey to comparatively few pests and diseases. It does not, for example, attract greenfly, whitefly, or blackfly. Nevertheless there are a few organisms that can, and from time to time do, attack begonias and growers must be alert to spot them so that early treatment can be given and the infestation localized.

Pests

Vine Weevil (Brachyrhinus sulcatus)

It is not the weevils themselves that cause the problem, but their white larvae. The parent weevils are very ordinary-looking, small, brownish beetles about $\frac{1}{3}$in (0.8cm) long which invade the greenhouse from time to time and lay their eggs on the surface of tubers and corms. When the larvae hatch, in early autumn, they burrow into the host tuber or corm, chewing their way voraciously through the tissues and becoming increasingly destructive as they grow in size. When begonia tubers are harvested neither damage nor grubs may be noticed, but one or two larvae can through the winter devastate a tuber to such an extent that it is useless when the time comes to start it into growth.

The best treatment is preventive. Water the plants from midsummer onwards with a proprietary insecticide, used at intervals according to the manufacturer's recommendations. Better still, incorporate an insecticide in the potting compost. Although Aldrin is available only to the commercial grower, there are plenty of other proprietary insecticides that are very suitable.

Nor must the parent beetles be ignored. During the summer they stay mostly outside the greenhouse and only come indoors as the weather gets colder. Ferns are especially popular host plants and any watering of begonias with insecticide should also include any ferns that happen to be in the greenhouse as well. Keep a sharp lookout for the beetles, destroy any you come across, and, having done so, take the hint by treating the plants with insecticide as soon as possible.

Thrip and Begonia Mite (Heliothrips haemorrhoidalis and Tarsonemus sps.)

Both these pests are extremely small; thrips are just visible to the naked eye, but mites require a magnifying glass for positive identification. Thrips leave brown streaks and trails on the underside of young leaves, especially along the veins, and on examination they can be seen as small, cigar-shaped, straw-coloured organisms moving actively on the surface. Mites mostly attack the growing points of shoots and can do enough damage to cause 'blindness' (that is, the refusal of the shoot to develop) or even the destruction of the growing point.

Fortunately both pests are susceptible to modern systemic insecticides. If damage from either is suspected, the whole plant should be sprayed thoroughly with a suitable proprietary product. Success will be evidenced in a very few days by the production of fresh, clean growth, but in any event a follow-up dose should be given after, say, a fortnight to deal with any pests that have hatched since the first treatment.

Eelworm

It is a general rule that the smaller the pest, the more difficult it is to counter; eelworms are very small indeed and extremely hard to eradicate. All eelworms are nematodes, that is, microscopic worm-like creatures that enter the plants, living inside them and eating away their hosts from within; because they live inside the plant they present considerable problems of control. There are two, perhaps three, forms that attack tuberous begonias.

The upper surface of a leaf affected by eelworm. The effects are first seen as areas of bronzing turning to brown and are bounded by the larger veins of the leaf. Eelworms are minute organisms, which easily pass from cell to cell, killing tissue as they go, but they seem reluctant or unable to cross the larger and presumably tougher veins. These areas of necrosis bounded by veins are typical of eelworm attack and enable speedy diagnosis.

The underside of the same eelworm-affected leaf; the symptoms are even more obvious on this side of the leaf.

Leaf eelworm (*Aphelenchoides olesistus*) restricts its activity to the foliage. The early symptoms are a darkening on the upper side of the leaf and a browning on the underside that reveal the areas of tissue damage; the areas are triangular and bounded by the main veins of the leaf, which the eelworms appear unable or unwilling to cross. Gradually the darkening on the upper surface gives way to brown and then to complete necrosis and withering. The triangular patches spreading to the edge of the leaf are very characteristic of this pest and enable early diagnosis to be made.

Tuber eelworm (*Meloidogyne sps.*), as its name implies, attacks the tubers and causes wart-like protuberances about $\frac{1}{4}-\frac{1}{2}$in (0.6–1.25cm) across to appear on the surface, usually in a cluster. These again are characteristic and easily diagnosed.

In addition to the above forms, there are also free-living nematode species which can exist outside the tissues of the plant and move around in a rudimentary way. One or more of these species may be responsible for a number of other conditions from which begonias suffer from time to time, among them being a distortion of the flower buds known as 'pimpling'. The 'pimples' are small pointed extrusions of the surface cells on the outer surface of the dorsal flower petals – the two outer petals that encapsulate the bud before it opens. Luckily the dorsal petals seem to protect the inner petals and these are rarely damaged. The eelworm species responsible for this distortion, if indeed it is an eelworm at all, has not been identified.

Until recently, plants attacked by eelworm were best destroyed on sight and any cuttings taken from them also destroyed – an effective method of control but a drastic one, especially as the pattern of eelworm attack seems always to obey Murphy's Law and to affect one's most-prized varieties and those of which one has least stock.

There are now three ways, in addition to the bonfire, of handling an eelworm attack. One is for the professional only and consists of treating the growing plants with the insecticide Aldicarb (formulated and sold under the trade name Temik) immediately the attack is noticed. Temik is a powerful and very dangerous agent and it is not available on the open market – indeed the mandatory precautions for even its professional use are most rigorous – but it can clear an eelworm infestation provided it is used strictly acccording to the manufacturer's instructions and within the imposed limitations; on no account should the amateur grower attempt to use this highly dangerous material despite the fact that, unfortunately, the usual run of proprietary systemic insecticides are of limited use in combating eelworms.

The second method of killing nematodes is by extreme heat. Excessively high temperatures over prolonged periods in the summer can break down plant tissue, and they have a similar effect on animal tissue as well. The trick, therefore, is to discover the temperature and time parameters or 'window' in which plant tissue will survive and the nematode tissues will not and to immerse the tubers accordingly in hot water at the appropriate temperature for the appropriate time. Trial and error indicate that tubers can be rid of eelworm completely by submersion at 49°C (120°F) for 30 minutes. This is higher than the usually accepted limit of 45.5°C (114°F) for 30 minutes, and readers wishing to use this method are recommended to carry out their own trials, bearing in mind that as the candidates for treatment are infected anyway they have nothing to lose by experimentation.

The third method of controlling eelworm, which is really an extension of good greenhouse hygiene and again more applicable to the professional than to any but the most dedicated amateur, is to water the plants only with totally pathogen-free water. This is achieved by passing the water first through a commercially-available device containing an ultra-violet lamp that kills not only eelworm eggs but also any bacteria that may be present.

Diseases
Powdery Mildew (Oidium begoniae)
Mildew is the most prevalent pathogen that attacks the tuberous begonia and it is difficult to eradicate completely once it has taken a hold. It is difficult to be specific as to the exact conditions which cause it and the likelihood is that the spores are in the air anyway and that luck plays a significant part in where they alight. However, there is no doubt that stagnant air pockets in the greenhouse and lack of air

Powdery mildew is first evidenced by the appearance of small white stars on the top sides of leaves. These quickly develop into small round, white patches, often likened to spots of cigarette ash, on the leaves. These spots quickly grow to cover the leaf surfaces. They are extremely unsightly and early treatment is essential.

movement around the plants provide the conditions that encourage the spores to settle and the fungus to spread once it has become established. Remarkably, the disease was unknown in Britain before 1953, but now it is widespread. Fortunately it can now be kept at bay, if not entirely eliminated, by preventive spraying. This should be carried out at regular intervals using a systemic fungicide such as Nimrod, beginning as soon as the plants are in their final pots and continuing until well into the autumn.

Powdery mildew first appears on the upper surfaces of the leaves as small 'stars', which quickly develop into white spots about $\frac{1}{4}$in (0.6cm) across that, once seen, are quite unmistakable. They should be wiped off immediately with cotton-wool soaked in fungicide, not forgetting to wipe the undersides of the leaves as well. Karathane is an effective preparation for this purpose because it clears up lesions that have already formed. It is less useful for preventive spraying, however, as it tends to burn the buds and flowers and it is not an easy preparation to handle, tends to clog spray filters, and leaves an unsightly deposit on the plants.

Stem Rot (Botrytis sps.)

Stem rot is indicated by a brown patch that appears on the side of the main stem, usually in the latter half of the season and especially among those plants that were started into growth early in the year. It is often traceable to excessive and probably unbalanced feeding, sometimes exacerbated by overcrowding of plants on the bench, which reduces the free flow of air around the plants. The patch increases in size quite rapidly, soon encompassing the stem and penetrating right through it. The brown tissue is soft and mushy and treatment, at least in the initial stages, consists of cutting away this soft tissue and wiping the wound firmly with a coarse rag, finishing off with a dusting of fungicide such as Karathane or Benlate, with repeated applications if necessary.

If the rot has spread right round the stem then major surgery will be required; the stem will have to be cut off just below the rot. Clearly, coming as it does with the plant in full leaf, this will at the least impose a shock upon the plant and, if the infection is low down on the stem, may leave it with only an inch or two of stem remaining. The priority, therefore, is to save the tuber for another year; all feeding must be stopped and great care taken to avoid overwatering until any new growth that may be produced from the tuber can get into its stride.

Tuber Rot

Rotting of part of the tuber may be discovered when it is being harvested at the end of the season. Almost always it is due to a secondary infection by fungal spores or bacteria after the tuber has sustained physical damage, perhaps through careless lifting or handling at some stage. Treatment consists of the excision of the rotted area, using a sharp knife so as to minimize further tissue damage, followed by dusting with Benlate or a similar fungicide.

Tubers which appear sound when harvested can nevertheless rot during winter storage, often shrivelling at the same time into hard lumps. This is almost invariably due to incorrect harvesting procedure, particularly to forcing the plant into premature rest.

Sciarid Flies

Also known as mushroom flies, these resemble very small houseflies. The flies themselves are quite harmless, but they lay their eggs on the surface of peaty composts and the small larvae feed largely on rotting vegetable matter. They are in fact also partial to very fine roots and can cause damage to seedlings for this reason. They are very easily killed by modern insecticides and flystrips impregnated with insecticide will keep them away.

Virus Diseases

It was fashionable at one time to blame any otherwise unexplainable plant condition on viruses. Thus begonia 'blindness', flower distortions, and many other growth oddities were all at one time or another laid at the door of the mysterious virus. Now we know better, and it is refreshing to be able to state that no known virus has been reported as attacking tuberous begonias. This is the more remarkable because the propagating knife has always been considered to be one of the main culprits in the passing of virus disease from one plant to another.

Miscellaneous Conditions

Corky Scab (Oedema)

This is a purely physiological condition manifesting itself, as its name implies, as a pale brown, scaly layer on the underside of the young leaves and along their stems. It is associated with poor root action, often but not always on recently started tubers, and should not be confused with the markings caused by thrips; corky scab is coarser in texture and covers areas rather than causing lines. The lack of root and top growth indicate an ailing tuber and it is best destroyed. Corky scab is not caused by or associated with any pest or disease.

Foliar Petals

This is a condition in which green, leaf-like appendages have been produced in place of the dorsal petals of flower buds, a bud having the appearance of a leaf at the back instead of a petal. They usually appear on the first one or two buds to be produced by the plant and subsequent flowers will almost certainly be normal. The condition is not caused in any way by pest or disease, seems to be more prevalent in white and yellow varieties, and is believed to be caused by too generous early feeding leading to lush foliage which 'spills over' into the flowers. Affected flowers should be removed at as early a stage as possible.

Flower Blotch
This is not an officially recognized condition, but is included because many growers become worried by the appearance on the flower petals of blotches of darker colour, uncharacteristic of the variety under normal cultivation. In the case of picotee-edged varieties, the phenomenon can take the form of the picotee edge 'bleeding' and extending towards the middle of the flower. Once this was blamed on the poor old virus, then on niceties of cultivation, but the real culprit, if that is the term, is the genetical make-up of the variety. It is a form of genetic breakdown which occurs in certain varieties from time to time. It is unsightly and spoils the flower for show, but there is no pest, disease, or physiological condition to blame and, because an affected plant may well produce entirely normal flowers in the following year, there is no reason for alarm nor for discarding the plant.

Soil Deficiencies
Such is the excellence of modern composts that the grower is unlikely to have to cope with conditions caused by lack of nutrients or trace elements in the soil. However, if symptoms of stunted growth or unusually coloured foliage extend throughout a batch of plants, a mineral deficiency of some sort must always be suspected. Fortunately treatment is very simple: watering with a chelated trace-element supplement will very quickly correct the deficiency and alleviate the symptoms. A general yellowing of

Begonia leaves are tender, and if they are exposed to direct sunlight without prior acclimatization (by increasing periods of exposure) they can suffer from sunburn. This takes the form of scorched stems and, as here, patches of brown, burnt tissue on the leaves. The plants are more prone to damage, and the damage is worse, if they are allowed to become too dry at the roots through inadequate watering.

the foliage often indicates magnesium deficiency; a condition which again can very easily be rectified by watering with magnesium sulphate, better known to most of us as Epsom Salts.

Scorching
Reference has already been made to damage due to scorching of the foliage of plants grown under glass. The symptoms are the appearance of burning or scalding of the leaves and the brown patches often cause growers to believe that their plants have contracted some serious disease. Excessive exposure to direct sunlight is responsible, however, and the damage is greatly increased if the plants are dry at the root and in need of watering at the time of exposure. Remedies for both causes are obvious.

7

GREENHOUSE MANAGEMENT

The art of growing good begonias – if it is a science at all it most certainly is not an exact one – is that of providing the optimum environment for the plants. In reality plants are not grown, they grow themselves, sometimes in spite of the treatment meted out to them, and what we call growing plants is in fact the provision of conditions in which they can develop without the checks to their growth that thoughtless handling sometimes causes. 'Green fingers' is really another name for an instinctive appreciation of the sort of treatment that enables plants to grow without hindrance and of the sort of growing conditions in which they will flourish.

The ancestors of our plants came from high-altitude rain forests and the conditions that prevail there are those they must have to give of their best and that we must try to emulate as best we can with our own individual resources.

The greenhouse – whether it be a traditional greenhouse, a conservatory, a garden room, or even a glassed-in patio or porch – should have provision for plenty of ventilation and preferably heating of some kind, though *not* by any gas-fired appliance. It should if possible be south-facing (in the northern hemisphere) and it should be as large as possible, because the problem will not so much be to keep the interior warm as to keep it cool in summer. Begonia tissues begin to break down at temperatures above 40°C (120°F) and the smaller the greenhouse the higher the temperature is likely to become. The greenhouse may be free-standing or a lean-to structure that will gain a little warmth in the winter from the building against which it stands.

Bound up with the matter of temperatures is the humidity. Begonias must have a high humidity at all stages of their growth if they are to flourish, and trying to grow them in a hot, dry atmosphere is doomed to failure. Provision of a high humidity in a propagator is one thing however, providing it in the open greenhouse in hot weather is quite another. For this reason it is good practice to spread a layer of gravel 2in (5cm) thick on the floor of the greenhouse under the staging and to keep it wet; the gravel acts as a humidity reservoir and the evaporation of the water from it helps to cool the air and keep temperatures within acceptable limits. Water should be splashed on the floor and staging as often as possible, twice a day in hot weather. (If the 'greenhouse' is a garden room containing furniture and upholstery it will be necessary to settle for standing the plants on trays of gravel that can be kept permanently wet.)

Tuberous begonias do not make good houseplants. This is for a number of reasons, chief among them being that the available light is insufficient to meet their needs and that the humidity in a dwelling house is far too low for them. Many is the plant, in full flower, that has been proudly taken into the house only to show its resentment of the move within a few hours by shedding its beautiful blooms one by one on the drawing-room carpet. Begonias drop their flowers when for some reason they are unhappy, whether because of overwatering, overfeeding, or a sudden move to a totally different and unsuitable environment; the effect is the same and disappointment on the part of the unsuspecting and, dare one say it, thoughtless, grower is intense. A favourite begonia can be shown off in the house, though, provided that it is placed on a tray of wet gravel to provide a humid microclimate around it and that it is taken back to the more congenial surroundings of the greenhouse within a few hours. There are plenty of begonias that make quite admirable houseplants, but, sadly, tuberous begonias, especially the large-flowered hybrid forms, are not numbered among them.

A lot of people who see begonias for the first time – and are ignorant of their Andean origin – believe that such exotic blooms must require enormously high temperatures and close conditions at all times. This is true at the early stages of seed-raising and tuber-starting, but the main problem in the summer months is that of keeping temperatures down to the 16°C (60°F) that the plants most appreciate. Splashing water on the floor and benches helps considerably but so too does adequate ventilation and it is a sad fact that many of the smaller, amateur greenhouse designs do not provide adequate facilities for good ventilation and air movement. The begonia house should provide ventilation both at low level and at or near the highest point, the theory being that as the air is heated it rises, escapes through the top ventilators, and is replenished by cooler air entering lower down. Draughts must of course be avoided at all times, but adequate free movement of air is essential for continued health and in particular the avoidance of those fungal diseases which are associated with stagnant air pockets, such as powdery mildew and stem rot. Free movement of warm, moist air around all the plants must be the aim and will be amply repaid by the performance of the plants.

In recent years, excellent ventilator control has been afforded by automatic devices which respond to temperature changes and open and close the ventilators as necessary. These are a boon during holiday periods as well as for busy amateurs who are quite unable to give the time they would wish to looking after their plants. They also afford a useful means of closing the ventilators at night, when the sudden chill after a hot day in early autumn can be harmful.

Another important aspect of proper environmental control in the greenhouse is shading from direct sunlight. The question is often asked, why, if begonias can be grown in the open without any form of shading, do they need it when they are grown under glass? The answer is that when sunlight penetrates glass it changes its character and contains more harmful, burning rays; it is quite different, as far as a plant is concerned, from sunlight outside. Begonias growing under glass should *never* be exposed to direct summer sunlight, but the more light they receive short of this the better and more balanced their growth will be. To provide these conditions artificial shading of some form or other is essential. This can take the form of a layer of white paint on the outside of the glass or some form of blind which can be drawn across over the plants, either inside or outside the glass. Paint, if used, should be applied early in the season, before the sun has built up its full strength, and be of the water-miscible type. It will be thinned by storms during the summer so that when the sun becomes less powerful again in the autumn its filtering effects will be appropriately reduced.

Better than paint, however, is a system of blinds that can be raised or lowered as dictated by weather conditions, either manually or, better still, by some form of automatic device controlled photo-electrically; such devices, though, are expensive for any but the smallest greenhouses. The best material to use is some form of man-made fibre, for strength and lasting qualities, and a coarse weave is best. This is because a coarse weave reduces the overall amount of light across the spectrum whereas a very fine one tends to reduce certain light wavelengths only. In recent years plastic films have been developed which greatly reduce the transmission of the harmful heat rays and can either be stuck to the inside of the glass or used in blind form. Although mainly used in building applications, there is no reason why they should not be equally suited to greenhouse shading.

Perhaps the best shading of all is by laths, often made of bamboo canes tied together and formed into mats. They are expensive, but they last for many years and, particularly in tropical and semitropical climes, are extremely popular. Indeed it is possible to grow begonias most successfully in lath-houses, which of course contain no glass at all, in those areas where heating is unnecessary.

Greenhouse hygiene aims at providing growing conditions in which pests and diseases have the minimal opportunity to flourish. First and foremost the greenhouse must as far as possible be free of pathogens at the start of the season, and this means cleaning it out properly during the begonias' winter dormancy. It means the generous use of greenhouse sterilizing agents to ensure that the staging and floor are properly clean and do not harbour insects or their eggs or fungal spores; it means using new pots each year and new seed trays; it means scrubbing those parts of the greenhouse that can be scrubbed – in short it means a lot of hard work.

During the growing season every dead leaf, every disbudded flower bud, and any other potential focus of rotting or possible hiding place for pests must be removed. It is thoroughly bad practice to leave detritus of this sort in the greenhouse; it should be removed and, preferably, burned. The stumps of old flower stems come into this category also; they should be left on the plant until they come away easily to a light touch and then be removed from the greenhouse.

The last chapter dealt comprehensively with the treatment of pests and diseases, but it must be stressed here that an eagle-eye must at all times be kept for the first signs of any attack. It is much easier and more effective to deal with pathogens and pathological conditions if they are spotted, diagnosed, and treated in the very early stages. It is even better, of course, to prevent their attacks by taking deterrent measures, such as regular spraying with fungicides, whether or not any mildew, stem rot, or similar 'nasty' is present.

The colour photographs that follow have been chosen primarily to illustrate the characteristics that distinguish flowers of high quality from their lesser cousins. A number of modern cultivars – both of large-flowered double begonias and of the graceful Pendulas – are shown and attention is drawn in the captions to their good or bad points. Most of these begonias are named varieties already in commerce, but some unnamed varieties that are not yet on the market or that have failed to make the grade are also included.

Other photographs show the conditions under which begonias thrive and some of the uses to which they can be put – growing in display houses, on their own and in company with other plants, in public parks, at flower shows, and adding colour to drab corners of the garden.

Finally, to remind us of the humble origins of modern tuberous begonias, we show several of their naturally occurring ancestors.

Unnamed double
A plant restricted to one stem does not necessarily bear only one flower at a time. Here no fewer than four blooms flower at the same time on the same stem, and all are in pristine condition. When begonia growers talk about 'good keeping qualities', they mean this ability of a flower to remain fresh-looking without deterioration at the edges even after being open for some time.

Nonstop begonias in an English park
The recently introduced Nonstop range is one of the very few F1 strains of tuberous begonias. The evenness of growth and uniformity of colour of the Nonstop begonias, which are bred primarily for bedding, make them ideal for massing together, especially as their parentage ensures that they begin to flower early in the season and produce a succession of flowers until well into early autumn. Here, in Victoria Park in the lovely English city of Bath, they are seen at their very best.

Bedding begonias in a trough
Because of their high flower-to-foliage ratio, large-flowered begonias brighten a dull corner most effectively. They are not usually regarded as suitable subjects for stone troughs, but in situations like this (*left*) they have much to offer.

Guardsman
It is often difficult to find a name for a new introduction, but 'Guardsman' was an easy and appropriate choice for this double begonia (*right*), which is one of the most brilliantly intense of the reds. The purist might perhaps consider, though, that its petals are too narrow for perfection.

Primrose
The delicate pastel-coloured flowers of 'Primrose' (*below*) are of impeccable quality and the plant is very vigorous – the flowers just keep on coming. Easy both to grow and to propagate, it is a great favourite.

Roy Hartley
'Roy Hartley' (*left*) is one of the great begonias of all time. Raised more than 20 years ago, it is the most sought-after variety there has ever been. It has probably won more prizes at flower shows than any other begonia of any sort. Among the reasons for its success are its large, profusely produced, and long-lived flowers.

Zulu
Richness and glowing intensity of colour – that make it seem as though the flowers are covered in velvet – give 'Zulu' (*above*) its distinction.

Tahiti

Every so often a new begonia is introduced that makes an immediate impact. One such was 'Tahiti' (*left*), whose attraction, especially to those exhibitors who like to display their flowers on boards, is its layer upon layer of broad petals, which, in a mature flower, can build up to a depth from front to back of more than 6 in (15 cm).

Fred Martin

The perfection of form and superb quality of 'Fred Martin' (*right*) are undeniable. Named after the late Secretary of the British National Begonia Society, it is in the opinion of many the finest picotee begonia yet raised. Note particularly the immaculate placement of the very broad petals.

Bali Hi

'Bali Hi' (*left*), a popular picotee-edged variety, is one of the very few begonias that vary slightly from plant to plant in their background flower colour – it may be pure white in one clone and pale cream in another. This is despite the fact that, like other named sorts, it is propagated vegetatively, which normally ensures that every plant of the variety is identical.

Coronet

The picotee begonia 'Coronet' (*above*) is little known. With its large, well-formed flowers it deserves to be more widely grown, but sadly it is difficult to propagate and will never be available in quantity, so it remains one for the connoisseur.

Apricot Delight

When 'Apricot Delight' (*right*) was first offered for sale by its raisers, in 1985, the laboratory to which it had been entrusted for tissue culture managed to lose all its stock, so, frustratingly, there were no plants to meet the first orders. Fortunately the raisers had retained a few tubers and were able to start again. This is a fine variety capable of producing huge flowers in an appealing, unusual shade.

Bernat Klein

If you wish to honour a brilliant fabric designer whose business is colour, you have to be careful when choosing a begonia to name after him, so a white-flowered variety seemed the safest choice. 'Bernat Klein' (*above*) is appropriately named also because of the heavy texture of its petals, which look almost as though they were made of damask.

Rosalind

The flowers of 'Rosalind' (*right*) are large but they tend to be too flat to win top honours and as a result the variety has never attained great popularity. It is worth growing, though, for its unusual colouring.

Allan Langdon
Named after the author's
father, 'Allan Langdon' is a
very easy-to-grow variety. Its
colouring is unusual – carmine
tinged with blue. See it against
a true, full-bodied crimson
and the difference is obvious.
The flower stems are long and
the blooms so heavy that
supports are necessary to show
them off properly.

Double begonias at the Chelsea Flower Show
Double begonias have long drawn dense crowds at London's annual Chelsea Flower Show. To get the plants in flower by mid-May, when the show is held, involves close attention and specialized growing conditions from the time they are started into growth in January right up until they are staged at the show. Before World War II, begonias at the show were staged on the ground, but post-war displays have been on tiered staging, as here. All the begonias here are single stemmed, but note the number of flowers on each plant.

Nectar

Some varieties, because of their unusual colouring, are difficult to categorize. One such is 'Nectar' (*left*), which is not a true picotee because its petals are on one side blush white and on the other a pale pink that sometimes spills on to the rims. Its delicate colouring has won 'Nectar' a wide following and has created a demand which its reluctance to produce more than a few cuttings has made difficult to satisfy.

Peach Melba

'Peach Melba' (*right*) was a popular variety in the fairly recent past, but, sadly, plants are now rarely seen. One of the characteristics that made it popular with exhibitors is its ability, when well grown, to build up layer upon layer of petals to give really spectacular blooms.

Avalanche

'Avalanche' (*left*) is popular because it is easy to grow, but it is characterized by flowers of rather thin texture.

Unnamed picotee
This (*top left*) is a very early picotee; it has flowers of good size and an abundance of petals, but very faint markings. From such unpromising beginnings (at least as far as markings are concerned) greater things develop – by hybridizing from weakly marked varieties like this and selecting from each generation those few seedlings that showed stronger markings than their parents, it has been possible, over many years, to create the range of picotees that we know today.

Sweet Dreams
'Sweet Dreams' (*bottom left*) produces large flowers of purest pink. Waved and crinkly petals add an extra dimension to the flower, especially when, as here, it has good depth and consists of many rows of petals.

Falstaff
Of the very few deep rose-pink begonias of high quality, 'Falstaff' (*above*) is the best. It was given its name because the rich colour of its flowers and its sturdy growth habit reminded the raiser of Shakespeare's character.

Unnamed double
This begonia was never named and never marketed, even though it produced flowers of supreme quality – note the depth of flower from front to back, the breadth of petal, and the perfect rosebud shape. Sadly, though, its production of cuttings left much to be desired and it became extinct before modern tissue-propagation techniques were applied to begonias. It proved an excellent parent, however, and so has lived on through its progeny.

Wedding Day
Although 'Wedding Day'
(*above*) has been superseded
by other, superior white-
ground picotees, it remains a
firm favourite because of its
sheer delicacy of colouring,
beautifully textured petals,
and overall flower quality.

Goldilocks
The intensity of colour that
can be achieved in the begonia
flower is evidenced by this
new variety, 'Goldilocks'
(*left*), soon to be released and
believed to be the most
brilliant yellow yet raised.

Bernat Klein
How wire flower supports can
be used to position individual
blooms of varieties with long
pedicels and heavy flowers,
such as this single-stem plant
of 'Bernat Klein' (*top left*).
Note the calluses in the leaf
axils at the bottom of the stem
where cuttings have been
taken.

Unnamed double
This unnamed variety (*left*)
has a flower of high quality
and good depth of colour. The
petals have crimped edges – an
unusual attribute that can be
most attractive.

Harlequin

'Harlequin' (*above*) created a sensation when it was introduced more than 20 years ago because of its wonderfully brash picotee markings – nothing quite like it had been seen before. The flowers are not numerous and the petal texture is by no means perfect, but the sheer exuberance of the colouring assures 'Harlequin' of a lasting place in the affections of countless enthusiasts.

Double begonias in the greenhouse

Although all plants benefit from having a greenhouse to themselves, and begonias are no exception, they are neighbourly creatures and their cultural requirements are sufficiently undemanding to make it possible to grow other plants harmoniously alongside them. A host of other plants will thrive under the same conditions, as is evidenced by this mixed display (*left*) in which the begonias are the jewels in the crown.

Midas

Finding names for new varieties is an important task for the raiser of any plant. Ideally, the name should give an idea of the colour or of an outstanding characteristic of the plant as well as being memorable. This yellow variety (*above*) with gently waved petals was named 'Midas', after the legendary king of Phrygia whose touch turned everything to gold.

**Begonia boliviensis and
Begonia pearcei**
Although they bear little
resemblance to the giant
begonias we know today, the
red *Begonia boliviensis* and the
yellow *B. pearcei* (*above*) are
two of the South American
species from which our
modern hybrids have been
developed. The weak-
stemmed, straggly *B.
boliviensis* is the ancestor of
today's Pendula begonias.

Begonia davisii
Begonia davisii (*above*), a
dainty little plant introduced
some 150 years ago at about
the same time as *B. boliviensis*,
is probably the species to
blame for the susceptibility to
powdery mildew of some
modern large-flowered
begonias.

Begonia veitchii
Begonia veitchii (*top right*) is in
many ways similar to *B.
davisii*, but it is a larger plant
with larger flowers borne on
stouter stems. It is of historical
interest only, as one ancestor
of the modern hybrids, and is
rarely seen outside botanical
collections.

Begonia pearcei
Begonia pearcei (*right*) is a
much more interesting plant
than *B. veitchii*. Not only is it a
worthy greenhouse subject in
its own right, but it is the
ancestor responsible for the
yellow colouring and the
attractive foliage markings
when they appear in modern
tuberous begonias. In recent
times it has been used as a
parent in experimental work in
the development of new types
of bedding begonias.

Unnamed double
The petal colouring of this unnamed variety (*above*) is unique in that it pales almost to white at the edges – a sort of reverse picotee effect. The flowers are a pronounced rosebud shape – a quality much prized by the experts.

Judy Langdon
Clear pink 'Judy Langdon' (*right*), although now quite elderly, is still very popular because of the large, crinoline-like flowers, with row upon row of petals, that it so reliably produces.

Unnamed double
Yet to be named, this double (*left*) may well become one of the all-time greats. The tomato-red colour is not unique, but the size and quality of the flower, the almost leathery texture of the petals, and the general bearing of the plant are all exceptional.

Pink Cascade

One of the finest of the modern Cascade Pendula begonias, 'Pink Cascade' (*above*) is not only remarkably free-flowering but also extremely compact in growth. The pendulous effect is the result of the sheer weight of the $3\frac{1}{2}$ in (9 cm) flowers coupled with thin, comparatively supple stems.

Irene

'Irene' (*left*), whose foliage reveals its likely descent from *Begonia boliviensis*, is one of the older types of Pendula begonias. Although these older types, with their small, dainty flowers, are far more graceful than the Cascade types in the early part of the season, they soon become thin and straggly and so have become less and less popular.

Fairylight

'Fairylight' (*right*) is one of the most popular of the picotee-edged varieties, and deservedly so – it has exquisitely modelled flowers with a milk-white ground colour and delicately profiled petals. It is a sister plant of 'Fred Martin' (see page 41) – that is, both come from same cross. It can be said perhaps that 'Fairylight' has inherited a classic colouring and 'Fred Martin' a classic shape.

Unnamed picotees

Picotees come in a range of different markings. The ground colour can shade from white through cream to yellow, while the edge markings may be either pink or red and can vary between the extremes of narrow rim and broad band. Picotees are among the most popular of all begonia types. The lovely white-ground picotee (*top left*), with excellent flower and petal form, and a sister plant (*above*) were raised from the same cross. Faced with such a choice, it is difficult for the raiser to decide which one to use for propagation.

Raised in 1967 but never marketed, this picotee (*left*) has the hallmark of an excellent begonia – a lovely deep flower with numerous broad petals. Sadly, though, the picotee markings are indistinct. In any case, this variety proved very difficult to propagate.

Very similar to 'Bali Hi' (see page 40) in colouring and flower form, this unnamed variety (*right*) was thought to be too close to an existing cultivar to be worth marketing. Had the centre of the flower been more rose-like the decision might possibly have been different.

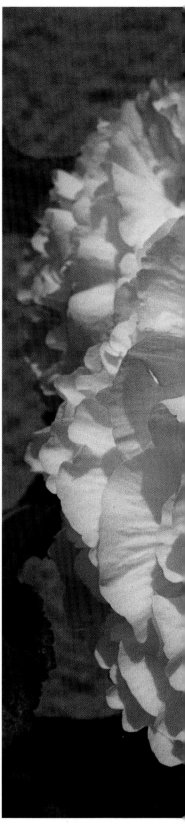

Unnamed double
More of a bi-colour than a
picotee, this unusual variety
(*above*) was discarded on
account of its flattish flowers –
a rather harsh judgement of a
kind that any raiser is
sometimes compelled to make.

Unnamed double
Not yet commercially
released, or even named, this
double (*right*) has the makings
of a real winner – very deep
flowers with wide petals,
attractively crinkled, and a
most unusual colouring.
Because of the way in which
the petals build up, layer upon
layer, as the flower develops,
this is a variety likely to
perform well as a cut flower
for exhibition on boards.

Rhapsody

'Rhapsody' is one of the really great begonias. Raised during World War II, it was, at one stage, lucky to survive, but it went on to become admired wherever it was grown for its ease of cultivation and the consistency with which it went on producing a succession of large flowers over a long period. It is a tolerant, undemanding, and much-loved begonia whose only disadvantage is that its long flower stems are often not strong enough to support the heavy flowers.

Hawaii
Quite how or why 'Hawaii' got its name is unknown – perhaps the rows of petals had connotations of grass skirts for the raiser. It makes a striking plant and has always been popular with exhibitors. Sadly, it is mean in the number of cuttings it throws and as a result stocks are always short.

Unnamed picotee
This is a yellow-ground picotee with little to commend it as far as shape is concerned but with good colour and unusually crisp markings.

Billie Langdon

The raiser, Stephen Langdon, thought this (*above*) to be the best white variety he had ever seen and named it 'Billie Langdon' after his wife. The white colour is of such purity that the backs of the dorsal petals in the flower buds, which in many varieties have a tinge of pink on them, are themselves an immaculate, unsullied white. This is a wonderful begonia.

Ken Macdonald

'Ken Macdonald' (*right*), an elderly variety, is seldom grown now that there are so many excellent modern orange varieties to choose from. Nevertheless, it was widely grown in its day – it was liked for its large flowers and clear colour and popular because it was easy to propagate and very reliable. It was named after a leading Australian begonia grower.

Lou-Anne

'Lou-Anne' (*left*) was one of
the earliest Pendula begonias
to have the now popular larger
flowers with rounded petals.
Raised in the United States, it
makes a compact plant (unlike
most early Pendula varieties,
which tended to very straggly
growth) and is (like most of its
type) very free-flowering. The
flowers are like small roses.
Although it has now been
around for a long time, it is
still widely grown.

Unnamed Pendula
This (*above*) was one of the
precursors of the Cascade
series of Pendula begonias.
The flowers were adjudged too
large and the stamens too
prevalent, but it proved to be a
useful parent in the
development of later types.

Orange Cascade
'Orange Cascade' (*right*) was
the first of the Cascade series
to be marketed. British bred,
the Cascade begonias are
descended from early
Pendulas that were crossed
with certain doubles with the
aim of enlarging their flowers
and compacting their growth.

Double begonias in the greenhouse
A fine show (*left*) of double begonias flowering in their prime. Note the slatted greenhouse staging to maximize the free movement of air around the plants and so minimize the risk of attack by such fungal diseases as powdery mildew and stem rot. This free movement of air does not encourage high humidity, so it is essential to keep the greenhouse floor well dampened.

Bedding begonias
A few begonias still bravely brightening a corner by a wall at the end of the season (*above*). These begonias may have no pretensions to flower size or quality, but they thrive with the minimum of attention in relatively indifferent conditions.

Melissa
'Melissa' (*left*) is a pure pink with a much paler centre – the opposite of the norm. The flower stems are short and strong, making external support unnecessary and giving the plant a compact habit.

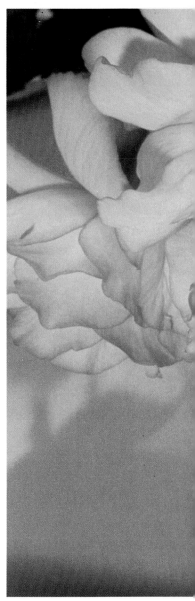

Apricot Cascade
Raised at the same time as 'Orange Cascade' (see page 73), 'Apricot Cascade' (*left*) is now rarely seen, despite the attraction of its unusual soft colouring.

Unnamed Pendula
Picotee varieties of Pendula
begonias eventually appeared,
as they had in double
begonias. This variety (*above*)
was one of the first. Its
markings are very faint, but it
proved useful for hybridizing
purposes.

Bridal Cascade
By far the best – and most popular – of present-day picotee Pendulas is 'Bridal Cascade' (*above*). A large hanging basket containing three or four plants of this variety will always attract admiring attention.

Unnamed double
In this unnamed double (*top right*) we see near perfection of flower form, with broad petals and central rosebud shape, combined with bold colour.

Lionel Richardson
A real old-stager is 'Lionel Richardson' (*centre right*), named after a famous Irish daffodil and narcissus raiser and keen amateur begonia grower. Its unusual colouring, ease of propagation, and general reliability ensured that it enjoyed a long commercial life.

Sea Coral
'Sea Coral' (*right*) has considerable show potential. Raised in 1980, it took almost a decade to accumulate sufficient stock to warrant its commercial introduction.

In the begonia house
The plants surrounding the
author in this greenhouse were
raised from pedigree crossings
made the previous October
and are those from which
selections will be made for
propagation as possible named
clones of the future.

8

SOILS AND COMPOSTS

Tuberous begonias are, in the main, extremely tolerant creatures and will grow and flower sometimes in seemingly very inhospitable conditions, but for them to give of their glorious best they have to have a well-developed and active root system; a soil or compost only provides the medium in which the latter can flourish. It must be both chemically and physically suitable for the purpose – chemically suitable in that it contains usable reserves of plant nutrients in a balanced ratio, and physically suitable in that it is absorbent but not too retentive of moisture, so that the roots can 'breathe' the air that is so essential to them.

Bedding begonias to a large extent have to put up with the available natural soil where they are to be grown, but even so attention to its preparation before planting will be amply repaid at flowering time (see page 14).

Potted begonias in the greenhouse, however, are entirely dependent on what their growers provide for them. In the past there were almost as many different mixtures as there were growers, each having his own closely-guarded pet formula to which he attributed his good results. The mystique grew and the best growers were accredited with adding some secret ingredient that alone was responsible for cultural success. Nowadays we recognize this folklore for what it was – pure nonsense – and while some growers continue to make up their own mixtures according to time-honoured recipes, most now use one or other of the modern loam-less composts consisting primarily of peat with added slow-release fertilizers.

Modern soil science could be said to date from the work carried out at the John Innes Horticultural Institute before World War II in a largely successful attempt to formulate a series of standardized potting mixtures that would suit the great majority of pot plants. Despite serious drawbacks, chief among them being that the loam that figured prominently among their ingredients was virtually impossible to standardize, the resultant J.I. Nos. 1, 2, and 3 composts found a ready acceptance among gardeners and, although they might now be thought a little outmoded, there are many who still use them today. They have, however, been outshone in recent years by peat-based composts, the current generation of which are well suited to begonia cultivation. One caveat must be given at this point; soil-less composts containing only peat and nutrients are likely to compact so tightly and retain so much water for so long that watering will be an extremely critical matter if the roots are not to sustain damage by the combined effects of prolonged contact with water and deprivation of air.

To overcome this possibility, growers should look for a peat compost containing a proportion of either coarse sand or one of the mineral additives, perlite or vermiculite. These 'open' the compost, enable it to drain more effectively, and hold some air at all times; by so doing they enable the roots to prosper as they should and make watering a much less critical operation. It is always advisable to check the acidity of the compost – a pH value between 6.5 and 7.0 is optimal, though there is tolerance between rather wider limits.

Begonias do not like too rich a compost – a fairly low level of immediately available nutrients is preferable, provided this is combined with a balanced slow-release formulation to sustain the plants as they grow. Of course even slow-release fertilizers will be exhausted before long, because vigorous plants just coming into flower at the height of the summer are at their most voracious, and supplementary feeding will be necessary, as we have seen (page 19).

Peat-based composts have one other drawback, especially if they are used in conjunction with plastic pots – that is, their lack of weight compared with soil-based composts in clay pots. We have seen that begonias are asymmetric in growth, having a 'back' and a 'front'. This gives them an inherent instability which becomes more and more pronounced as flowers are produced, until they can easily topple over. Careful staking of the plant, and support of the flowers, will normally solve the problem.

Now that excellent soil-less composts are freely available in garden centres and shops, recommendations for suitable formulations for the basic composts will not be given here, but the following fine-tuning suggestions and observations may prove helpful. First of all, though, a word of caution; if peat is allowed to become *really* dry, its structure is such that it is almost impossible to wet again, at least in the short term. Water runs off bone-dry peat rather like quicksilver and is not absorbed. The better-quality composts contain a wetting agent, which helps to overcome the problem, but it is better that the compost should never be allowed to get so dry.

For starting tubers and potting: use one of the proprietary soil-less potting composts either on its own or with the addition of up to one quarter its volume of perlite or one third its volume of medium-grade vermiculite.

For seed-sowing: use one of the proprietary soil-less seed composts either on its own or with the addition of up to half its volume of fine-grade vermiculite.

For rooting cuttings: use one of the proprietary soil-less potting composts with the addition of up to half its volume of either perlite or medium-grade vermiculite.

If buying proprietary J.I. mixtures, it should be understood that the quality of the mixture is only as good as the quality of the individual constituents, and especially that of the most variable – the loam. The name John Innes implies only that the ingredients are mixed in the recommended proportions, it does *not* guarantee the quality of those ingredients.

9

PENDULA BEGONIAS AND OTHERS

Pendula Begonias

The so-called Pendula or hanging-basket begonias have long been great favourites of the gardening public. They are eminently suited to growing not only in the many forms of hanging container but also in ornamental urns and vases, large terracotta pots, and other containers – anywhere in fact where their pendulous form can make an impact.

There do not appear to be any records covering the very early development of Pendula begonias, once known collectively as *B. lloydii* after one of the early pioneers, but it is generally accepted from their comparatively slender stems and habit that *B. boliviensis* figures predominantly in their family tree, and indeed some of the very early double varieties were later reclassified as Pendula types because their stems, while 'thin, weak, and drooping' for double begonias, became 'graceful and arched' for Pendulas. A weak, drooping stem is a prerequisite for any Pendula, because the pendulous effect depends on the weight of the flowers pulling them over the side of the container.

In essence, therefore, a good Pendula begonia should have thin but wiry stems producing a multitude of flowers. At least three stems should be allowed per tuber and, apart from the first flower buds, which should be removed to build up the strength of the plant, all the flowers, both male and female, should be encouraged because it is the mass of flower that is important rather than the size or form of individual flowers.

Until the last ten years or so Pendula begonias mostly had flowers with thin, narrow petals giving the effect of multi-pointed stars, but more recently the Cascade series has appeared with rounded petals that give the flowers the look of a small-scale double-begonia and with somewhat stiffer main stems. They were pioneered by Reinelt in California and arose from crossing the traditional types with carefully selected large-flower double forms and have found much favour with the public, especially the latest picotee-edged forms.

The culture of the Pendula types closely follows that for double begonias, with seeds being sown and tubers started in exactly the same way. The only major difference is that, whereas the shoots produced by double begonias are restricted to one, or at the most two, all the shoots produced by Pendula begonias should be encouraged. When the shoots are about 3in (7.5cm) tall the plants should be transferred to the basket or vessel in which they are to flower, using one of the potting media already described. A small – up to 10in (25cm) diameter – vessel will accommodate three one-year-old tubers of the old-fashioned, starry-flowered type of Pendula begonia or one of the newer Cascade type; a 12–15in (30–40cm) diameter vessel will need four and two respectively. Needless to say, if the plants are destined for outdoor decoration they should be hardened off beforehand as already described for bedding begonias (page 14), while supplementary feeding will likewise follow the guidelines already laid down (page 19).

No description of Pendula begonias would be complete without mention of the scented varieties 'Yellow Sweetie' and 'Orange Sweetie'. Both are

One of the newer Cascade types of Pendula begonia – here just coming into flower.

extremely difficult to propagate and as a result are rarely to be seen in catalogues, but 'Yellow Sweetie', with its lemon-scented, primrose-coloured flowers, deserves a place in every collection.

Multiflora Begonias

The original Multiflora begonias, thought to be derived from *B. davisii* and *B. pearcei*, are small-flowered varieties originally raised in Belgium and until the last twenty years widely grown there. They are named clones and were propagated vegetatively by the hundreds of thousands in the area around Ghent for sale for bedding purposes all over the world. The best known are 'Flamboyant' (red) and 'Helen Harms' (yellow), introduced in 1911 and 1902 respectively, but they are extremely labour-intensive to propagate and have gradually been superseded by the seed-propagated strains of Multi-flora Maxima, developed and introduced by Deiner in Germany in the 1950s and soon sold in large numbers. Whereas the majority of the original Multifloras bore flowers of single form, the Maximas have double flowers, about 2in (5cm) in diameter, produced in profusion over a long season. A few

selections are separately named, prominent among them being 'Schweizerland', a bedding subject remarkable for its unique combination of rich crimson flowers with very dark, almost brown, foliage.

Bertini Compacta Begonias

This group consists of a range of compact-growing begonias not unlike the Multiflora Maximas but with single flowers, averaging 2–2$\frac{1}{2}$in (5–7.5cm) in diameter, produced in even greater profusion. They are seed propagated, are ideal for massed bedding, and have much charm. In spite of their name, they are not closely related, if at all, to the straggly early hybrid *B. bertini* and do not resemble it.

Nonstop Begonias

Much intensive breeding work in Europe in recent years has resulted in the introduction of a number of new F1 strains of tuberous begonias from crosses between the large-flowered double types and the new forms of Multiflora Maxima. Chief among the newcomers is the Nonstop series, a range of extremely floriferous begonias with flowers smaller than the average double begonia but with the mass of bloom associated with the Multiflora Maximas. They possess an abundance of hybrid vigour but do not compare with the large-flowered, double clones for greenhouse cultivation.

Other Forms and Types

The types described above represent macro-divisions of *B. tuberhybrida*, which historically had well-defined boundaries even if some of these are now becoming somewhat blurred as a result of recent hybridizing between types. There are also what can be called micro-divisions within the large-flowered double-begonia group. These include the following:

Camellia and Rose-form Begonias

These are really two different forms of the double begonia and are a legacy of the very early development days when there were two different types – those with a small, rather flat centre giving the appearance of a camellia and those whose centres were prominent and rose-shaped. Nowadays the distinction is academic and the boundary impossible to define, but the names are still sometimes found.

Picotee Begonias and Bicolours

These again are subsections, modern this time, of the double begonia; they differ only in their colouring. Picotees can have a basic colouring of either yellow or white, with petals outlined with narrow edges of pink or red. They differ from bicolours in the width of the contrasting petal rim – if it is narrow then it is a picotee, if wide a bicolour, but here again there are borderline cases between the two. In both types the additional modelling that the edging confers on the flower greatly enhances its attractions and both forms are extremely popular.

Marginata, Crispa, and Crispa Marginata Begonias

The marginata begonias are to picotees what single-flowered begonias are to the double forms; they can be described as single begonias with picotee markings. The crispa forms are self-coloured and have deeply frilled edges to the petals. The crispa marginata types combine the coloured edge with the frills

and are sometimes known as Fascination begonias; all three types are museum relics nowadays, though they do appear from time to time.

Marmorata Begonias

Marmorata begonias enjoyed a fleeting popularity a few years ago and are still to be found in some collections. The double flowers are predominantly red in colour, heavily blotched with white, and rarely of good quality.

Fimbriata or Frilled Double Begonias

Another variation on the double-begonia theme, the flowers this time having serrated petals giving the appearance of very large carnations. While in the case of the picotees the contrasting edging of the petals gives modelling to the flower and enhances quality, the fringing of the fimbriatas, which varies from slight frilling to deep serrations, blurs the modelling and in the opinion of many tends to detract from the formal shape and quality of the flower. Fimbriata begonias have little public following.

Single Begonias

At the turn of the century single begonias were as widely grown as the early double forms, if not more so, and it is sad to think that after developing along parallel tracks for many years there is no quality strain extant. A good-quality single flower with two broad dorsal petals 7in (18cm) across and two secondary petals only a little smaller was, even in the days of perfectly shaped and larger double forms, still a delight to behold – it had a purity of form and a dignity lacking in other types. The few singles that are to be seen nowadays are, sadly, mere shadows of their illustrious ancestors.

Crested Begonias

Sometimes also known as bearded begonias, these extraordinary types are of single form with tufts of frilly petal tissue attached in the middle of each of the four petals. They were remarkable more for their grotesque shape than for any pretensions to quality or even beauty. Apart from a brief resurrection in a seedsman's catalogue a few years ago, crested begonias enjoyed little popularity and are believed to be extinct.

IO

EXHIBITING BEGONIAS

Although there are many enthusiastic amateur growers who revel in the disciplines of cultivating and preparing their begonias for exhibition purposes, they are massively outnumbered by those who grow them simply for greenhouse decoration and their own pleasure and delight. All growers wish to realize as much of the potential of their begonias as they can and it is worth emphasizing that they will get from their begonias in proportion to the time and effort they are prepared to put in; there are no secrets and no short cuts. Professional growers win prizes because they devote their working lives to growing their chosen speciality; they are on hand to take corrective action if they notice anything amiss and they have the resources immediately available to cope with most eventualities.

Provided the grower has given the necessary attention to detail in the growing of his plants they should provide him with high-quality – even show-quality – flowers. Most growers will be content with this, but for those who wish, or are persuaded, to compete there follow some tips and observations that may prove helpful.

First, read the show schedule carefully. This seems a very obvious instruction, but there is nothing more frustrating than taking one's pride and joy to the show bench only to have it rejected by the judges as 'Not according to schedule'. Study the schedule, therefore, and decide which class you wish, or have the ability, to enter. In general there are two groups of begonia classes – for plants, and for flowers only. The former are judged as well-flowered, well-grown, and well-presented plants.

The latter are exhibited on 'boards' – flat surfaces inset with small glass or metal water-containers which hold the flower stems so that the flowers lie on the board, which is usually held at a slight angle to the horizontal to improve presentation. There may be classes for single plants and groups of three or six plants (or even more in large shows) and for single flowers, and three, six, or twelve flowers. Make your choice and do not get carried away by the number of plants or flowers you think you will have available – remember that you will almost certainly fall short.

Growing for plant classes and growing for flower classes require different techniques. A good plant, as we have seen, must be well furnished with as many good-quality flowers as possible, while for flowers on boards large size and freshness are very important. Whether there is more skill required in growing for plant or for individual flower excellence has long been debated, but what is not in doubt is the fact that flowers on their own are very much easier to transport to a show than grown plants well furnished with flowers. Sadly, what is also undeniable is that once shorne of its flowers for showing on a board a begonia plant is not the most attractive sight in a greenhouse.

We have dealt already with the techniques involved in growing good plants and mention has been made of producing specimen plants from large tubers which produce more than one shoot, but while, other things being equal, a specimen plant with two stems will carry more weight with the judges than one grown on a single stem, other things very rarely are equal, and a well-grown plant on a

86

single stem will always be given precedence over one with two spindly stems.

When growing for board display, the size and general condition of the plant itself takes second place to the flowers. The selected plant should be single-stemmed. Academically speaking, all buds but one should be removed; in practice it is safer to allow two buds to remain, in case timing is badly judged or adverse weather conditions intervene. At this point also the plant (unless it is a variety prone to produce double centres) should be 'stopped', that is the growing point of the stem should be removed by bending it gently back until it snaps. Stopping channels the resources of the plant away from foliar growth and into the flowers. Unfortunately, varieties liable to produce poor-quality centres will be encouraged in this bad habit by stopping and this is one reason why some varieties are known to be better for showing as flowers on boards and others as plants. Experience is the only guide.

Correct timing is all-important and, while certain parameters can be laid down, much will depend on the variety and on weather conditions and only experience can provide the final judgement. Timing can be divided into macro-timing and fine-tuning timing; the former is concerned with when to start the tubers into growth in the spring and the latter with subsequent disbudding.

The important season for flower shows is the six-week period from the middle of July to the end of August and for plants to be at their peak during this time they should be allowed at least four and a half to five months' growth. This means that they should be started into growth in late March or early April at the latest. Turning to fine tuning during the season, we have seen that the begonia produces a succession of flowers and if the early ones are removed, as they should be, succeeding ones will be that much bigger and of much better quality. The reason for this sort of disbudding is to build up the resources of the plant before flowering, but this property of successive flowers being produced is most helpful also because it allows us to plan and to a large extent control the flowering season. As a general rule, therefore, it can be stated that a flower bud 1in (2.5cm) in diameter will take six weeks to reach its peak, so that by disbudding over a period until, six weeks from the show, the buds are of this size they should be in prime condition 'on the day'. However, *this is only a guide.* Trial and error is the only way to take account of individual varieties, local conditions, and so on and a dummy run is strongly advised.

Showing is demanding of time and effort and is not for everyone, but there is no reason why all begonia growers should not strive towards show quality in their plants even if they never actually reach the show bench.

The Perfect Begonia
Anyone with any pretensions to exhibiting begonias will want to know what the judges will be looking for – what are the qualities of a good begonia? A similar question will be asked by those interested in hybridizing – what are the qualities for which one should be breeding?

The Flower
There are four things to look for in a high-quality begonia flower – depth of flower, breadth of petal, texture of petal, and flower-shape. Thus the flower must have good depth (from front to rear), preferably about 1in (2.5cm) less than the diameter, with the individual petals at least 2in (5cm) and preferably 3in (7.5cm) wide – narrow or pointed petals give a thin, mean look to the flower. The texture of the petals must be as heavy as possible – in the sense that a silk might be described as heavy. This is a quality difficult to describe but immediately recognizable when one comes across it. The flower should have a good complement of petals, but not appear too crowded. The centre should resemble an opening rose from which the layers of petals gradually blend one into the other towards the back of the flower. There should be no marked gap where some layers have pulled back to leave a gap and give a 'cup-and-saucer' effect, with the centre of the flower, the 'cup', pointing forward away from the reflexed rear petals, the 'saucer'. Flowers opening to a muddled or multiple centre are not acceptable.

Size of flower is also important, but, within limits, must always take second place to quality. If other things are equal, the larger the flower the more highly will it be rated, but size alone must never be allowed to take precedence over quality.

However excellent it may be in other ways, no flower can be considered perfect if it does not possess good keeping qualities, and judges will always award points for freshness. The ideal should be that individual flowers should last in good condition until such time as other flowers on the same plant have opened, so that a number may be fully open on the same specimen plant together.

The Tuber

Tuber size alone is no criterion of excellence; it is possible to grow top-quality plants from comparatively small tubers. In practice, though, larger tubers are easier to keep during the winter because they suffer less from shrivelling or shrinkage.

The Plant

The most important characteristic of any plant is that it should be possessed of vigorous growth. Inherent vigour in plants usually accompanies the fringe benefits of ease of cultivation and propagation, together with – most importantly – an above-average resistance to disease. For this reason the pursuit of vigour should figure prominently in any long-term breeding programme. Thus varieties that give only the occasional cutting, are temperamental in their growth, or require constant attention should not be used as parents *however outstanding their flower quality*. Many otherwise exquisite types have been discarded because their propagating potential was too low to be commercially viable.

Begonias as cut flowers

One of the bonuses offered by the tuberous begonia is the fact that its flowers last surprisingly well in water. They need to be placed in water within a few seconds of cutting to avoid the formation of air locks in the fleshy stems, but if this is done and they are allowed to absorb water for an hour or so, they will then stand several hours out of water without flagging, a useful trait if they are to be transported, for example, to a show. In the home they are both decorative and a major talking point as the centre-piece of a dining table, perhaps floating in a crystal bowl or arranged in a brandy glass or silver chalice. In any room in the house, though, begonias arranged with skill and artistry in a suitable, perhaps shallow, container make a sensational display.

Another use to which they can be put is in the preparation of wedding bouquets. Not the large double flowers – few brides would welcome them – but the much smaller flowers of the Pendula varieties, and perhaps some of the single female flowers. After that all-important initial drink after cutting they should easily last for the rest of the day and provide a delightful and most unusual feature of the wedding accessories.

The cut-flower potential of the begonia has never been exploited to the full in Britain, but in the United States of America, especially on the western seaboard, cut begonias are extremely popular and are sold extensively in florists' shops, where they regularly command good prices.

II

HYBRIDIZING BEGONIAS

The creative urge exists in every one of us and in the begonia enthusiast it sooner or later takes the form of a wish to raise new varieties. That can be a very satisfying pastime, absorbing and at times exciting, but it can be frustrating and disappointing when things do not go as hoped. Unfortunately there are a number of characteristics peculiar to the begonia that tend to restrict serious hybridizing to the professional. This is not to say that the keen amateur should be discouraged, merely that he should be aware of the difficulties and not set his sights too high.

To begin with, certain characteristics of the begonia require consideration. First, as we have seen, the male and female sexes are carried in different flowers, though on the same stalk from the main stem. The flowers are produced in threes; the central flower is always male, one of the others is always female, and the third may be either male or female. Female flowers are always single in form and each bears its triangular shaped seed-box behind the petals; male flowers are much larger and are, in double begonias, of double form. Hybridization consists of the transference of pollen from the stamens of a male flower on to the stigma of the female. There is no problem about this with the species, all of which have single flowers with a clump of stamens in the middle, with old-fashioned single begonias, which are likewise well endowed, or with poor-quality semi-double flowers. With all of these there is pollen available for the taking. But what of the large-flowered, modern double forms with their high-quality flowers and not a pollen grain, nor even

Hybridizing consists of the transference of pollen from a selected male flower to a female flower. The best means of carrying out this operation is to use a small paintbrush, preferably of sable-hair.

a stamen, in sight? Where do we find our pollen? For an answer to this we have to look at what 'doubling' means in a flower.

Begonia flowers of single form all possess the central bunch of stamens which give rise to pollen grains as they ripen, rather like miniature seed pods. More petals arise, over many generations, by the modification of these stamens into extra petals, leading eventually, through semi-double forms, to completely double flowers in which there are no stamens, and therefore no pollen, at all. We have seen that our 'perfect' flower is fully double with a rose-bud centre, and the paradox therefore emerges that as we breed and select over the years for ever more 'perfect' flower form, so we are at the same time breeding out the ability to produce the pollen we need to further our programme. Fortunately, all is not lost because nature steps in at this point and enables at least some of the better-quality flowers to produce pollen *under certain circumstances*.

Just as other members of the plant kingdom tend to produce seed more readily and in greater quantity under adverse conditions, so begonias that under good growing conditions produce large, fully double flowers can often be persuaded to produce pollen if they are grown under conditions of semi-starvation at the end of the season. This is best achieved by allowing cuttings taken during the earlier part of the season to remain in small pots so that they become starved and produce pollen. This is normally around October, which, by happy coincidence, is the optimum seeding season.

Another factor to be taken into consideration is that begonias are particularly susceptible to the debilitating effects of inbreeding. These do not become apparent in the course of two or three generations and so are unlikely to affect the amateur grower, but for the professional specialist who has to consider a programme over a period of years this is a very real problem. For this reason the introduction of new blood into a strain is of particular importance, and all commercial plant breeders have trial grounds where they can grow strains and varieties of other specialists' raising to compare with their own and to act as a nucleus source of breeding material for hybridizing purposes. Of course, not all such material will be sufficiently worthy to cross with one's own lines, but experimental crosses of this kind must feature in all long-term programmes if the vigour and well-being of a strain is to be maintained.

One point often overlooked but which should be considered by budding hybridists at an early stage is the amount of room that the seedling progeny will occupy in the greenhouse and garden. The actual pollination process up to the point at which the seed is harvested takes up very little, if any, extra greenhouse space, but after seed-sowing and up to flowering the plants demand an ever-increasing amount of room. One pod of seed can yield several hundreds of seedlings. Even if these are planted out at the bare minimum of 10in (25cm) apart each way they still take up a lot of space in a small garden. So the amateur should go for quality of cross rather than quantity and flower only a given number of plants from each cross, say a maximum of two dozen, enough to give an idea of the potential of a cross. If the quality proves outstanding the cross can always be repeated in the following year.

So select your parents carefully, using the best possible material, and duly make your crosses, remembering that as each separate pollen grain equates to one seed, the more pollen transferred and the more evenly it is distributed on to the stigma of the female flower the greater will be the yield of seeds. A useful tip is to select as female parents only those varieties that have short and compact stigmas and styles (the style is the thick tissue between the stigmatic surfaces and the seed box). The reason for this is that the pollen grains have to germinate on the stigmas rather as seeds do on compost and grow down all the way into the seed box, and this seems to be too much for them if the styles are too long. The best instrument to use for transferring the pollen is a small artist's paintbrush, preferably of sable-hair, because the pollen clings more readily to this, although camel-hair will do. After making each cross always dip the brush into methylated spirit to sterilize it, and allow it to dry before using it again.

A few days after pollination the margins of the stigmas will begin to turn a pale brown, a sure sign that pollination is under way. After a week or so the triangular seed box should be examined daily for signs of withering. The green sides will gradually turn brown and become thin and papery and small cracks will appear near the stem. At this point the pod should be picked and laid on a saucer, in subdued sunlight if possible, to dry. After a further few days the cracks in the skin will widen and the seeds may be shaken out and cleaned; this is easily done, but great care must be taken to ensure that the very small and light seeds do not spill. Along with the good seeds there will always be a proportion of chaff. This can be removed by blowing it away *very lightly and very carefully* and then turning the residue on to a sheet of white cartridge paper and slowly inclining it so that the good seeds run back into the saucer leaving the small amount of residual chaff clinging to the matt surface of the paper. Repeating this several times will complete the cleaning to professional standards.

Finally the seeds may be stored in a small, waxed paper envelope in a refrigerator, though of course not in the freezer, until the time comes to sow them.

12
BEGONIA MILESTONES

Over the years, there are some varieties that stand out as possessing that little extra that lifts them above their contemporaries, be it a colour break, unusual stamina, overall quality, lasting ability, or just extreme popularity with the amateur grower. In charting these I have not gone back to the very early days, but have tried to draw the line so as not to exclude any variety that might, even in this day and age, still be grown somewhere.

Strangely enough, the early varieties of Pendula begonias have remained in commerce far longer than their contemporary large double-flowered types. The orange Pendula variety 'Mrs Bilkey' was offered in a 1909 nursery catalogue and still listed by the same company in the early 1970s. The most famous of all the pre-World War I Pendula begonias, the aptly named 'Golden Shower', was introduced in 1912 and there are plants still in existence today. It is a notoriously late variety to start into growth, but remarkable in that winter dormancy losses hardly ever occur. More recently, the pale pink 'Lou-Anne', which originated in the United States, heralded the introduction of the Cascade series of larger-flowered Pendula varieties that are so popular today.

Among double-flowered tuberous begonias, the following are worthy of inclusion in any roll of honour; they are listed in chronological order of introduction.

In 1923 two varieties were introduced that were certainly head and shoulders above what had gone before – 'Hilda Langdon' and 'Lord Lambourne'. 'Hilda Langdon' was named after the younger daughter of the raiser and was a pale rose-pink.

'Lord Lambourne' was salmon-orange in colour and named after the then President of the Royal Horticultural Society. It is interesting to note that one was described as having a "perfect rose shape" and the other a "perfect camellia shape" (see page 85).

The late 1920s and the 1930s saw many fine varieties being introduced. One of them was the great white begonia, 'Everest', introduced in 1934, which in those days produced flowers described as being 'frequently of 8in diameter'. It was pure white with a multitude of slightly waved petals and was an instant success. Over the years, its flower size and vigour have gradually fallen away, but it was still being offered in the late 1970s and no doubt there are many tubers giving yeoman service to this day.

'Rhapsody' was released in 1948. It was another instant success and there are many tubers of it still in the hands of amateur growers, though it is true to say that its original vigour has now become somewhat depleted. The flowers were pure rose-pink and very large, but above all it was a superb plant for beginner and expert alike as it was so easy to grow and so generous in its production of flowers. It had one vice – its flowers were so heavy that the stems were incapable of holding them upright – but countless aspirants to show honours cut their exhibition teeth on it and it served them well.

Another, and quite different breakthrough, 'Hercules', came in 1950. 'Hercules' was an apt name – it was in every way a real giant of a begonia, 'Was' rather than 'is' because sadly time has taken its toll and the original vitality of the variety has been sapped. In its heyday, in experienced hands, it won just about every prize going in show classes for 'one tuberous begonia, any size of pot'. It was a begonia with (almost) everything, huge flowers, lots of them, and a vigour of growth unmatched before or since. It made tubers so enormous that it could be grown not just on one stem, nor on two, but on *three* stems if circumstances allowed. Hopefully there are one or two tubers still in existence, but if not it certainly leaves a wealth of memories.

The year 1961 produced an exceptional wine vintage in Bordeaux and an exceptional begonia vintage in Bath. 'Roy Hartley', named after a much-loved north-country doctor, had originally flowered some years earlier but it first 'went public' in 1961. It was destined to become one of the best known and most widely grown of all the large-flowered hybrids. Equally suitable for growing as a specimen plant or for individual cut flowers, it is an all-time great and likely to continue in popularity for many years yet.

Among begonias with picotee markings, once again a very few stand out from the crowd. 'Harlequin' in 1964 and 'Wedding Day' in 1971 both had red markings on a white ground colour, while 'Corona' in 1968 was equally outstanding among those with a yellow ground colour. Indeed 'Harlequin' must be one of the most popular named double-begonia varieties ever raised; would that stock of it in quantity was available today!

SOURCES OF QUALITY STOCK

Virtually every nursery shop and garden centre sells 'begonia tubers' in the early spring, most of those offered in Europe being of Belgian origin and most of those on sale in North America coming from California. These are the mass-produced tubers, raised and sold in their millions and representing, for the prices asked, excellent value for money. They have been bred for even-ness of colour and growth and above all for size of tuber; for massed bedding purposes they are colourful and reliable, but for sheer quality and size of flower they do not compare with those that have been bred with different goals in view. For the more discriminating grower – the enthusiast for whom only the best is good enough – the following sources are recommended:

Blackmore & Langdon, Pensford, Bristol, BS18 4JL, England.
T. White & Son, Park Mains Nursery, Inchinnan, Strathclyde, Scotland.
Antonelli Brothers, 2545 Capitola Road, Santa Cruz, CA 95060, USA.
White Flower Farm, Litchfield, CT 06759, USA.

RECOMMENDED MODERN VARIETIES

The varieties recommended here should remain both easily available and at or near the top of their colour range for some time to come, but it is with the caveat that no variety will last for ever that they are suggested. They have had to bear close scrutiny both on ease of cultivation and general reliability, and are listed in their colour groups.

Red

Sceptre A dazzling scarlet variety with row upon row of lightly frilled petals.
Zulu Very deep crimson in colour with good shape and medium-size flowers. (See page 39.)

Pale Pink

Judy Langdon Pale sugar-pink with very many rows of petals which allow the flowers to build up considerable depth, especially when grown under cool conditions. This characteristic makes it particularly popular for display on boards. (See page 61.)
Sugar Candy Slightly deeper in colour than 'Judy Langdon', and with more than a hint of salmon in the colouring. The flower stems are shorter than usual and so stiff that support for the flowers is never required. A very easy and rewarding variety for the newcomer to exhibition begonias.
Roy Hartley Salmon-rose in colour with flowers so heavy that in order to display them at their best they must be given support. They are produced in profusion and are exceptionally long-lived. (See page 38.)

Rose Pink

Falstaff Very rich, almost glowing, rose-pink colour producing large flowers. The growth habit is very compact. A disadvantage is that propagation is slow as it throws few side shoots. (See page 51.)

Yellow

Festiva Introduced over twenty years ago, this is now rather long in the tooth, but is included here because it is easy and reliable. The shade is an intense chrome yellow and it is very floriferous, though by modern standards the flowers are only of medium size.
Primrose Pale, slightly luminous flowers with a hint of a green tinge. When this variety is good, it is very, very good. The petals are broad and the flowers have fine, rose-shaped centres. It is easy to propagate. (See page 37.)
Buttermilk A rich cream shaded – and occasionally blotched – with palest pink. It can scarcely be called yellow, but it is difficult to know how else to classify it. It produces comparatively few, very large flowers and is remarkable for the leathery texture of its petals.

White

Bernat Klein It bears enormous, almost cabbagy flowers, with slightly waved petals, which take on a tinge of cream towards the centre as they mature. A fine, 'gutsy' variety. (See pages 44, 54.)
Billie Langdon The purest white imaginable. Very recently introduced, it has a classic begonia shape and smooth-textured petals. Stephen Langdon, now in his eighties, has named it after his wife and regards it as the pinnacle of a life spent cherishing his chosen flower. Remarkably, it is easy to propagate, being very generous in the production of cuttings. (See page 70.)

Orange

City of Ballaarat This might seem a strange name for a begonia, but begonias are well known in Australia and especially so in Ballaarat, where the City's Parks Department has large greenhouses devoted to them and holds an annual Begonia Festival complete with Begonia Queen. 'City of Ballaarat' produces large flowers. The colour sometimes appears blotched.

Tahiti A vibrant shade that is very difficult to describe, though tangerine is probably nearest. This is another variety that is suitable both for growing as a specimen plant and for individual cut-flowers. The flower builds up layer after layer of petals and keeps in good condition for days – a very useful trait if showing is in mind. (See page 40.)

Picotees

Fairylight and **Fred Martin** Sister plants raised from the same cross, but they are both outstanding in rather different ways. 'Fairylight' has smoother petals, milky-white in colour with a narrow but well-defined red rim, while 'Fred Martin', named after the much-respected late Secretary of the National Begonia Society, has heavier petals, slightly waved, with a cream ground colour and again a striking red rim. (See pages 41, 63.)

Can-Can There have been a number of picotees with a strong yellow ground-colouring to the petals, but apart from 'Corona', and now 'Can-Can', few have had the inherent vigour to merit inclusion here. 'Can-Can' is a very strong-growing begonia and a comparatively tall one, and with its large flowers with their bright red rims perhaps a more apt name would be 'Marmalade'.

These then are a selection of modern double tuberous begonias. They are all capable of giving a good account of themselves on the show bench, but they are first and foremost plants that may be grown for pleasure by the amateur gardener.

BEGONIA SOCIETIES

Keen amateur growers may wish to join one of the several specialist begonia societies that afford the opportunity to meet and correspond with enthusiasts throughout the world. The names and addresses of the honorary secretaries of three of these are:

The National Begonia Society: Dr Eric Catterall, 3 Gladstone Road, Dorridge, Solihull, West Midlands, B93 8BX, England. (This society covers England and Wales.)

The Scottish Begonia Society: Mrs I. Hendry, Clydebridge Lodge, Greenacre Estate, Motherwell, Strathclyde, Scotland.

The American Begonia Society: Jeanette Gilbertson, 410 Joann Circle, Vista, CA 92084, USA.

BIBLIOGRAPHY

Bedson, F. J., *Successful Begonia Culture*, Collingridge, 1954

Brown, Worth, *Tuberous Begonias*, Barrows & Co., 1948

Catterall, E., *Growing Begonias*, Croom Helm, 1984

Coates, A. M., *The Plant Hunters*, McGraw Hill, 1969

Genders, Roy, *Begonias*, Gifford, 1958

Haegeman, J., *Tuberous Begonsias; Origin & Development*, Cramer, 1979

Langdon, Allan, *The Tuberous Begonia*, Mendip Press, 1949

Langdon, Brian, *The Tuberous Begonia*, Cassell, 1969

Otten, George, *Tuberous Rooted Begonias & Their Culture*, de la Mare Co., 1935

Thompson, M. L, & E. J., *Begonias, The Complete Reference Guide*, Times Books, 1981

Wynne, B., *The Tuberous Begonia, Its History & Cultivation*, Gardening World, 1888

Most of these works are currently out of print. Wynne's book is included because of its drawings of the Andean begonia species and early hybrids. Haegeman's book is a very worthwhile scientific survey and Mr & Mrs Thompson's work is a remarkable illustrated treatise on all known begonia species, forms, and hybrids (to the date of publication). The other books listed are all, in their different ways, rewarding, interesting, and informative.

INDEX

Apr/90
Mc...tiel